Embracing Culturally Responsive Practice
in School Libraries

American Association
of School Librarians
TRANSFORMING LEARNING

EMBRACING
CULTURALLY
RESPONSIVE
PRACTICE
in School Libraries

ELISABET KENNEDY

ALA Editions

CHICAGO | 2023

ELISABET KENNEDY works as a school librarian at a high school in New Jersey. She graduated with a bachelor of arts degree in English and journalism media studies from Rutgers University, went on to earn her master in library and information science degree from San José State University, and most recently earned a master of arts degree in education from Marshall University. She values continuous professional growth through studying and implementing inclusion and representation initiatives in school libraries, understanding and improving user experience, and learning from antiracist/antibias practitioners. She is a proud Latina, wife, homebody, thyroid cancer survivor, pop culture fangirl, and local cuisine enthusiast.

Extensive effort has gone into ensuring the reliability of the information in this book; however, the publisher makes no warranty, express or implied, with respect to the material contained herein.

ISBN: 978-0-8389-3862-1 (paper)

Library of Congress Cataloging-in-Publication Data
Names: Kennedy, Elisabet, 1993- author.
Title: Embracing culturally responsive practice in school libraries / Elisabet Kennedy.
Description: Chicago : ALA Editions, 2023. | Includes bibliographical references and index. | Summary:
  "This guide will help translate pedagogical principles into practical school library strategies for you to
  implement as you move through the continuum of cultural competence and build a culturally
  responsive school library space"—Provided by publisher.
Identifiers: LCCN 2022050582 | ISBN 9780838938621 (paperback)
Subjects: LCSH: School libraries—United States. | Culturally relevant pedagogy.
Classification: LCC Z675.S3 K45 2023 | DDC 027.80973—dc23/eng/20230113
LC record available at https://lccn.loc.gov/2022050582

Book design by Alejandra Diaz in the Utopia Std and Galano typefaces.

♾ This paper meets the requirements of ANSI/NISO Z39.48-1992 (Permanence of Paper).

Printed in the United States of America
27 26 25 24 23   5 4 3 2 1

V, thank you. You are my calm.
You are my home. You are everything.
I love you. E.

CONTENTS

PART IV

EVALUATION 73

ACKNOWLEDGMENTS

To my parents and brother: Gracias por darme una vida llena de amor. Tu amor, fe y apoyo me guía en todo lo que hago. Los amo cada dia mas.

To my husband and family: Thank you for your outpouring of love and support. You all make my days brighter, my life fuller, and my heart happier.

To my friends: Thank you for accepting me into your lives with huge hearts and open arms. You are inspirations.

To my editors Jaime Santoro, Stephanie Book, and the whole ALA Editions team: Thank you for approaching this project with patience and kind hearts. You molded my big ideas into something worth sharing, and for that I am forever grateful.

To my fellow librarians: Thank you for changing lives every day.

INTRODUCTION

Welcome to *Embracing Culturally Responsive Practice in School Libraries*. You are taking the first steps in exploring the ever-evolving road of culturally responsive practices as they relate to school library services. You are taking ownership of your profession, the role you play in your school, and, as a result, the impact you have on learners' lives.

Follow me throughout this guide as we translate pedagogical principles into practical school library strategies for you to use right away and others that will grow with your practice. You can continue to promote literacy, increased access to information, inclusive practices, equity, and equality through your work while taking meaningful steps toward a culturally proficient mindset. Keep in mind that there is no end goal to be reached; instead, being a culturally proficient leader, school librarian, and educator is a journey. Use this guide to continue learning and working through changes as you move through the continuum of cultural competence, discussed later in this introduction. Building a culturally responsive-sustaining school library space takes time but will prove invaluable to your work and your learners and will help solidify the school library as a community space within the school.

In this introduction, we will begin with an overview of the philosophy and principles behind culturally responsive-sustaining pedagogy and related evolving pedagogies/practices. Then we will turn to the connections between culturally responsive-sustaining pedagogy and our work as school librarians. Finally, we will end with a look at the *AASL Standards Frameworks Applied to Culturally Responsive Practice*.

Culturally Responsive Teaching Practices

School districts across the country are emphasizing culturally responsive teaching practices in the classroom. This teaching philosophy celebrates how learners' cultures shape everything from their communication habits to how they process information. As information centers and community hubs, school libraries are in an ideal position to align with culturally responsive teaching principles to provide expansive resources and brave spaces for librarians, other educators, and learners. As school librarians, you already possess the innate instincts to do this work, but understanding where it all began and why it matters will give you a solid foundation for your exploration of cultural proficiency.

To guide your exploration, it is important to understand the terminology and context behind culturally responsive-sustaining pedagogy. The terminology listed in the following section, coupled with foundational principles, will give you the tools to understand, reflect, discuss, apply, and share with confidence.

Terminology

Culture: "the set of practices and beliefs that is shared with members of a particular group and that distinguishes one group from others" (Lindsey et al., 2019)

Cultural proficiency: "a tipping point from viewing cultural differences as deficit-based to learning how to value cultural differences as assets on which educational experience are built" (Lindsey et al., 2019)

Cultural proficiency continuum: "provides language to describe unhealthy and healthy values and behaviors of persons and policies and practices of organizations. Additionally, the continuum can help you assess your current state and project your desired state. Movement along the continuum represents a paradigmatic shift in thinking from holding the view of tolerating diversity to transformative action for equity" (Center for Culturally Proficient Educational Practice 2020)

Culturally responsive pedagogy: "using the cultural characteristics, experiences, and perspectives of ethnically diverse students as conduits for teaching them more effectively" (Gay 2002)

Culturally sustaining pedagogy: "requires that our pedagogies be more than responsive of or relevant to the cultural experiences and practices of young people—it requires that they support young people in sustaining the cultural and linguistic competence of their communities while simultaneously offering access to dominant cultural competence" (Paris 2012)

Implicit bias: "Also known as unconscious or hidden bias, implicit biases are negative associations that people unknowingly hold. They are expressed automatically, without conscious awareness" (Staats 2012)

Sociopolitical consciousness: "the ability to take learning beyond the confines of the classroom using school knowledge and skills to identify, analyze, and solve real-world problems" (Ladson-Billings 2014)

Breaking It Down

If you are encountering these big concepts and terminology for the first time, I'm here to lend a hand. This book will not shame you or make you feel like you aren't doing enough. Instead, we will work together to bolster your confidence, expose you to a useful reflective practice, and help you create intentional and impactful change in your school's culture. Now, when we speak of culture and the other concepts explored, we want to lean on the definitions just shared. Using a shared terminology will not only keep us on the same page but also allow for deeper understanding and exploration. Culturally responsive practices become easier to digest when you break them down.

Culture, as defined previously, is "the set of practices and beliefs that is shared with members of a particular group and that distinguishes one group from others" (Lindsey et al., 2019). Every person has a culture they belong to or identify with. Understanding culture is made easier when it is described in layers. Figure 0.1 illustrates these three layers as "surface," "shallow," and "deep" (Hammond 2015).

FIGURE 0.1

Culture chart

	Surface Culture	Shallow Culture	Deep Culture
Hammond's Collective Qualities	Talk styles, cooking, holidays, songs, art, language, music, hairstyles, food, clothes, games, drama, literature, stories	Concepts of time, acceptable food sources, personal space, eye contact, ways of handling emotion, nature of relationships, tempo of work, being honest, nonverbal communication, theories of well-being and diseases, child-rearing principles	Decision making, concepts of self, worldview, definition of kinship, cosmology, spirituality and concept of a higher power, relationship to nature and animals, preferences for competition or cooperation, notions of fairness
Hammond's Collective Properties	Observable patterns, low emotional impact on trust	Unspoken rules, high emotional impact on trust	Collective, unconscious beliefs and norms, intense emotional impact on trust
School Library Applications	Display books and resources with varied characters and themes, responsive signage, use community vernacular	Guide in authentic reflection, social and personal identity activities, embrace vulnerability through sharing, provide actionable feedback, opportunities for constructive conversations	Embrace learner identities, reflect on inquiry process and bias, opportunities for learner feedback on policy and programs, encourage learner choice in collaborative work, be mindful of family structures and communication
School Library Properties	Visible inclusion, shared understanding, welcoming environment, increased access to multiple perspectives	Intentional connections, affirming dialogue, partnerships with accountability, shared norms for behavior and discussions	Shared ownership over space and services, regular incorporation of reflection, learner voice is empowered, responsive methods of communication

Source: Adapted from the Culture Tree model created by Hammond (2015).

FIGURE 0.2

Cultural proficiency continuum for school libraries

Reactive ◄──────────────────────────────► Tolerance		
Cultural Destructiveness	**Cultural Incapacity**	**Cultural Blindness**
"Seeks to eliminate the cultures of others in all aspects of the school and in relationship to the community served"	"Trivializes other cultures and seeks to make the cultures of others appear to be wrong"	"Choosing to ignore the discrepant experiences of cultures within the school"
School Library Adaptation		
Actively alienating and excluding learners' identities and experiences with language and policies. "This is America. We only need books in English."	Devaluing certain groups and providing fewer resources and materials based on deficit thinking. "Don't worry about those kids. They don't read anyway."	Providing culturally irrelevant resources and materials to the school's population; assuming that everyone's needs are the same. "We are all the same."

"Surface culture" describes shared interests in music, literature, celebrations, holidays, clothing, art, food, and the like. If you can't readily identify your culture, this may be a great place to start. Your favorite sports team, your pop culture fandom, the food you and your family enjoy, state- or citywide celebrations—these are all examples of culture. Surface culture offers an accessible layer to explore when incorporating culture in the school library. The types of interests in this layer can be easily highlighted within your school library space.

"Shallow culture" describes shared, unspoken rules regarding eye contact, personal space, handling emotions, the nature of relationships, and so on. Nonverbal communication is a valuable currency in our society. One false move like avoiding eye contact or speaking too loudly can easily lead to feelings of disrespect, distrust, or resentment. In considering this layer, we want to think of expectations that we have of others that aren't expressed in our written rules or policies. For example, you have the expectation that your desk is off limits to learners and other educators, but if your personal office supplies go missing, your expectation was not met. Though the importance of personal space is not explicitly stated in our day-to-day encounters, it is an essential piece of feeling safe and secure. Another example of expectations about personal space comes into play when communicating with parents. If a parent is opposed to shaking your hand or offers an unexpected embrace when first meeting, that action may offer the opportunity to explore a cultural difference.

Proactive ◄─────────────────────────────────────► Transformative		
Cultural Pre-Competence	**Cultural Competence**	**Cultural Proficiency**
"Increasing awareness of what you and the school don't know about working in diverse settings"	"Personal values and behaviors and the school's policies and practices [are] aligned in a manner that is inclusive of cultures that are new and different from yours and those of the school"	"Advocate for lifelong learning for the purpose of being increasingly effective in serving the educational needs of cultural groups in your school and community"
School Library Adaptation		
Highlighting a variety of identities and cultures in book displays and booklists. "Representation in literature matters."	Evaluating and modifying policy and collection to improve inclusivity; reaching out to communities for insight. "Leaning into learning."	Embracing learning opportunities to continually gain deeper understanding of culturally responsive and antibias work. "I *am* an advocate."

Source: Adapted from Lindsey et al. (2019, table 7.1).

"Deep culture" is much more emotionally charged than the others. This layer describes collective, unconscious beliefs and norms. Here we find notions of fairness, competition/cooperation, mental health, concepts of self, spirituality, and the like. Those notions influence how we make sense of the world, take in information, make decisions, and problem solve. This layer can range from something as simple as assigning group work instead of individual work depending on learners' comfort to more emotionally complex situations like being mindful of family structures or pronoun usage. We may not reach this layer easily in the school library space, but this layer of culture is vital when understanding ourselves and others. Deep culture offers an opportunity to further analyze where our unconscious beliefs seep into our practices, policy making, and instruction in order to enact meaningful change.

Understanding the different levels of culture allows us to then explore our viewpoints regarding culture and how we integrate it into our school libraries. The continuum of cultural competence is a tool we can regularly visit to evaluate our mindset and actions throughout this journey (figure 0.2). Adopting culturally relevant practices will shift your mindset and move you from wherever you find yourself on the continuum toward cultural proficiency. One day you may identify with the Cultural Pre-Competence space on the continuum, and the next day you may identify with the Cultural Incapacity space on the continuum. It is a fluid, introspective, and situational process. Cultural proficiency is "a tipping point from viewing cultural differences as deficit-based to learning how to value cultural differences as assets on which educational experiences are built" (Lindsey et al., 2019). That said, it is essential to remember that the "tipping point" does not equal the end point. Being intentional with your actions and holding yourself accountable through the culturally responsive lens requires dedication, honesty, a willingness to change, and a commitment to reflective practices.

Once we better understand what our cultural identities are, we can start to appreciate the cultures within our schools and those of our learners and colleagues in a deeper sense. Whether we can pinpoint the exact ways in which we incorporate the different layers of culture into the school library space or we are just starting our journey on the continuum of cultural competence, the framework and scenarios in this book will highlight opportunities for culturally responsive practices in our school library spaces.

Laying the Foundation

In this section, we will briefly explore the work of those who laid the foundation for culturally responsive-sustaining pedagogy, cultural critique, and reflective practices in the school setting. The philosophies of the following scholars influence the strategies that will be discussed in the framework and throughout the chapters. Though there is a lot of information to grasp, preparing for our journey with the proper context is important. With each highlighted scholar, I hope to offer an introductory view of the pedagogies and practices that influence our exploration. The purpose of this book is to translate these essential principles into strategies relevant to your school library practice.

Geneva Gay

In her book *Culturally Responsive Teaching: Theory, Research, and Practice* (2002), Geneva Gay noted that culturally responsive teaching is culturally validating and affirming. It has the following characteristics:

1. Acknowledges the legitimacy of the cultural heritages of different ethnic groups, both as legacies that affect students' dispositions, attitudes, and approaches to learning and as worthy content to be taught in the formal curriculum
2. Builds bridges of meaningfulness between home and school experiences as well as between academic abstractions and lived sociocultural realities
3. Uses a wide variety of instructional strategies that are connected to different learning styles
4. Teaches students to know and praise their own and each other's cultural heritages
5. Incorporates multicultural information, resources, and materials in all the subjects and skills routinely taught in schools

Ana Maria Villegas and Tamara Lucas

In their *Journal of Teacher Education* article, "Preparing Culturally Responsive Teachers: Rethinking the Curriculum" (2002), Ana Maria Villegas and Tamara Lucas noted that culturally responsive teachers possess six distinct characteristics:

1. Sociocultural consciousness: Recognizing that there are multiple ways of perceiving reality and that these ways are influenced by one's location in the social order
2. An affirming attitude toward learners from culturally diverse backgrounds: Seeing resources for learning in all learners rather than viewing differences as problems to overcome
3. Commitment and skills to act as agents of change: Seeing themselves as responsible for and capable of bringing about educational change that will make schools more responsive to all learners
4. Constructivist views of learning: Understanding how learners construct knowledge and being capable of promoting learners' knowledge construction
5. Learning about students: Knowing about the lives of their learners
6. Culturally responsive teaching practices: Using their knowledge about learners' lives to design instruction that builds on what learners already know while stretching them beyond the familiar

H. Samy Alim and Django Paris

In their book *Culturally Sustaining Pedagogies: Teaching and Learning for Justice in a Changing World* (2017), H. Samy Alim and Django Paris noted that culturally sustaining pedagogy requires the following:

1. Instructional practices that are more than responsive or relevant to the cultural experiences and practices of young people
2. Support for young people in sustaining the cultural and linguistic competence of their communities while simultaneously offering access to dominant culture competence
3. The explicit goal of supporting multilingualism and multiculturalism in practice and perspective for learners and educators
4. Linguistic, literate, and cultural pluralism as part of the democratic project of schooling

Randall B. Lindsey, Kikanza Nuri-Robins, Raymond D. Terrell, and Delores B. Lindsey

In their book *Cultural Proficiency: A Manual for School Leaders* (2019), the authors noted that the following essential elements are an interdependent set of standards that guide your being intentional while on your journey toward cultural proficiency:

1. Assess culture: Claim your differences.
2. Value diversity: Name the differences.
3. Manage the dynamics of differences: Frame the conflicts caused by differences.
4. Adapt to diversity: Change to make a difference.
5. Institutionalize cultural knowledge: Train about differences.

In the School Library

The evolutions of culturally responsive pedagogy apply seamlessly within the school library space. As school librarians, we already take learners' shared experiences, emotional and educational needs, and identity into consideration. With data, school librarians can assess gaps and use our expertise when providing instruction and resources. We decorate our space and engage with learners, but there is always room for more substantial engagement through intentional actions and reflection. This book will empower you, through introspective approaches to pedagogy and thoughtful research in culturally responsive work and inclusive school library practices to shake up some, but not all, of your methods and perhaps even your own mindset. The techniques in the applied framework (figure 0.3) and throughout the chapters should be jumping-off points, not set accomplishments that are guaranteed to succeed or check off the culturally proficient boxes. Take the techniques and mold them into feasible approaches that make sense for you and your school library program. Be willing to work through discomfort and know that support is out there, if not in your own room or building then throughout this guide and in the network of school librarians exploring this practice. There will be barriers in this work, like time, resources, support, and even our own hesitations, but my hope is that our journey will equip you with the tools to overcome those challenges and build a sustainable practice.

AASL Standards Frameworks Applied to Culturally Responsive Practice

Figure 0.3 applies the AASL Standards Frameworks in the *National School Library Standards for Learners, School Librarians, and School Libraries* (2018) to culturally responsive practice. This applied framework will provide you authentic perspectives and AASL Standards–based strategies that will guide your practice, influence your policies, and strengthen your school library's impact. The purpose of integrating culturally responsive practices into our day-to-day school library work is to foster a learner-centric, individualized, inclusive learning environment. Fortunately, our profession naturally encourages our commitment to the representation and affirmation of various racial, linguistic, and cultural identities. Building on that encouragement with deeper understanding and actionable strategies, we can lean into culturally responsive principles to intentionally and authentically develop our skills in ways that enhance our school libraries.

We will explore reflective strategies that rely heavily on vulnerability and challenge us to discover and share more about ourselves. We will also encounter opportunities to empower learners to share their voices and those of historically marginalized figures. Let the framework act as a support beam as you continue on this journey. Throughout the book, direct references to points within the applied framework will be marked by parentheticals denoting the AASL Standards Shared Foundation and Domain along with the culturally responsive practice or activity being referenced. For example, the parenthetical (figure 0.3, I.B.P2) indicates Inquire/Create Practice 2, and (figure 0.3, I.B.A1) indicates Inquire/Create Activity 1. Approach the challenges, reflective exercises, and activities with an open mind. I hope that the ways in which you incorporate the various methods are as unique as your school library and the communities within it.

FIGURE 0.3

AASL Standards Frameworks applied to culturally responsive practice

	I. INQUIRE	II. INCLUDE	III. COLLABORATE
A. THINK	**PRACTICES** 1. **Learners display curiosity and initiative by:** Privately identifying personal identity, prejudices, and perspectives. 2. **School librarians teach learners to display curiosity and initiative when seeking information by:** Identifying shared and differing cultural reference viewpoints on respect, authority, praise/shame, and collaboration.	**PRACTICES** 1. **School librarians direct learners to contribute a balanced perspective when participating in a learning community by:** Evaluating school library policy and educator/volunteer training documents to pinpoint areas for culturally relevant improvement. 2. **The school library supports balanced perspectives through resources and learning opportunities by:** Identifying increasing and decreasing cultural population trends school-wide and among library users.	**PRACTICES** 1. **Learners identify collaborative opportunities by:** Identifying and reflecting on viewpoints presented by learning groups that challenge personal perspective. 2. **The school library facilitates opportunities to integrate collaborative and shared learning by:** Encouraging partnerships with public libraries and community groups to increase access and ideas.
A. THINK	**ACTIVITIES** 1. Expand instructional scope using periodic reflections of our own identities and those of learners—for example, by using surface culture for context, such as interests, traditions, and celebrations. 2. With learners, cocreate norms for brave and respectful conversations in the school library, which can be useful when reviewing material and guiding general conduct.	**ACTIVITIES** 1. Use a sample of learner data, like cultural backgrounds, interests, sociopolitical context, and relevance, to examine school library policies for inclusive practices, outdated expectations, and unnecessary boundaries. 2. Include a small group of learners in evaluation of policies, increasing learner agency and ownership in the school library space.	**ACTIVITIES** 1. Introduce a "new to me" anonymous whiteboard, forum, or document where learners can share new perspectives gained from peers' presentations/work. 2. Explore public library offerings, services, and books for each age group to expand your own knowledge base and better serve the school's learners, educators, and families.

	IV. CURATE	V. EXPLORE	VI. ENGAGE
A. THINK	**PRACTICES** **1. Learners act on an information need by:** Analyzing personal search impulses and reflecting on strategies that can be further modified, replaced, or developed. **2. School librarians challenge learners to act on an information need by:** Promoting credible information sources that learners may not be regularly exposed to, such as different nonprofit organizations and advocacy groups.	**PRACTICES** **1. School librarians foster learners' personal curiosity by:** Reflecting on personal bias, previous reactions to challenging situations, and resource selection. **2. The school library supports learners' personal curiosity by:** Reflecting on the role of safety, bravery, inclusivity, and intellectual challenge in the school library space.	**PRACTICES** **1. School librarians promote ethical and legal guidelines for gathering and using information by:** Incorporating the issue of censorship into digital literacy lessons and explaining its role in the scope of ethics and ideologies. **2. The school library serves as a context in which the school librarian ensures that the school community is aware of the guidelines for safe, ethical, and legal use of information by:** Understanding the technological equipment available to learners at home by using district data and small-group surveys to maximize school library impact.
A. THINK	**ACTIVITIES** 1. Reflect on information-gathering habits with learners, opening a discussion about personal preference, interest in the topic, challenges, and learners' first impressions about the topic. 2. Gather lesser-known credible sources and display them continuously in person and on an updated digital document, exposing educators and learners to possible areas of interest and advocacy.	**ACTIVITIES** 1. Study the cultural proficiency continuum and reflect on your current position on the continuum, knowing that the continuum is fluid and meant to inspire engagement and motivation. 2. Explore the creation of safe and brave spaces as appropriate for your school library.	**ACTIVITIES** 1. Expand the scope of Banned Books Week into a true exploration of censorship and the ideologies behind the actions. 2. Conduct a technology needs assessment of the school library space, highlighting points of concern, learner needs, and service gaps.

(cont'd)

FIGURE 0.3

AASL Standards Frameworks applied to culturally responsive practice (cont'd)

	I. INQUIRE	II. INCLUDE	III. COLLABORATE
B. CREATE	**PRACTICES** **1. School librarians promote new knowledge generation by:** Prompting learners to reflect on the information they gather. Before an assignment, learners can pinpoint their preconceived notions about the topic and plan their course of action. **2. The school library enables generation of new knowledge by:** Engaging in practices that make resources accessible in and outside the school building, with minimal to no barriers to access.	**PRACTICES** **1. Learners adjust their awareness of the global learning community by:** Understanding differing perspectives and biases through digital literacy. **2. School librarians establish opportunities for learners to adjust their awareness of the global learning community by:** Evaluating the school library with culturally responsive principles in mind.	**PRACTICES** **1. Learners participate in personal, social, and intellectual networks by:** Becoming increasingly comfortable with experiencing and working through discomfort when collaborating with other learners and other educators. **2. The school library's policies ensure that school librarians are active participants in development, evaluation, and improvement of instructional and program resources with the school community by:** Understanding how learners are affected by policies and procedures to better defend, modify, and overhaul existing agreements.
B. CREATE	**ACTIVITIES** 1. Guide learners though the adapted KWWHL Chart and a reflection on the different sections. 2. Utilize online portals, digital classroom forums, and social media to increase access and promote services for learners and educators.	**ACTIVITIES** 1. Expand digital literacy to examine the current state of news media by studying media bias and the importance of differing perspectives. 2. Engage in regular evaluation of the school library space through the lens of differently abled, multilingual, and traditionally marginalized learners.	**ACTIVITIES** 1. Emphasize learner choice as a fundamental part of instruction while mandating changes in group makeup per task to increase diverse perspectives and approaches to topics discussed. 2. Highlight specific areas in need of modification within policies to share with the school community. This strategy will help control the influx of perspectives while still encouraging and fostering collaborative spirit.

	IV. CURATE	V. EXPLORE	VI. ENGAGE
B. CREATE	**PRACTICES** 1. **Learners gather information appropriate to the task by:** Constructing an effective and efficient process for critically examining information resources. 2. **The school library promotes selection of appropriate resources and tools for information use by:** Inviting learners to act as advisors about the materials in the room and to digitally document any resource reviews.	**PRACTICES** 1. **Learners construct new knowledge by:** Fostering exploration by openly welcoming mistakes and sharing successful problem-solving strategies. 2. **The school library facilitates construction of new knowledge by:** Exposing learners to different types of content and learning experiences through a multitude of learning environments or stations within the school library space.	**PRACTICES** 1. **School librarians act as a resource for using valid information and reasoned conclusions to make ethical decisions in the creation of knowledge by:** Emphasizing constructive and direct feedback cycles. 2. **The school library supports ethical processes for information seeking and use by:** Embracing culturally responsive school year celebrations through displays, booklists, and lessons.
B. CREATE	**ACTIVITIES** 1. Safeguard the school library and school librarian from resource challenges with an approved policy, direct learner involvement and engagement in materials selection, ALA talking points, and community partnerships with the public library. 2. Evaluate learners' selections and newly constructed processes to pinpoint gaps and bridges.	**ACTIVITIES** 1. Invite vulnerability by discussing common missteps and the importance of trial and error in the research process. This approach will build a trusting exploratory environment and allow you to connect with learners on a personal level. 2. Involve learners in peer teaching models to showcase learners' previous knowledge and their abilities to teach others using their own peer-to-peer, culturally relevant language and approaches.	**ACTIVITIES** 1. Use feedback to facilitate conversations and partnerships with learners. 2. Create and continually modify a culturally responsive school library calendar to help keep important cultural, book-related, and library-related celebrations at the forefront. This increased awareness will influence your book displays, booklists, lessons, and programming.

(cont'd)

FIGURE 0.3

AASL Standards Frameworks applied to culturally responsive practice
(cont'd)

	I. INQUIRE	II. INCLUDE	III. COLLABORATE
C. SHARE	**PRACTICES** 1. **Learners adapt, communicate, and exchange learning products with others in a cycle that includes:** Sharing information-gathering methods and thoughtfully reflecting on how and why the sources were selected. 2. **The school library provides learners opportunities to maintain focus throughout the inquiry process by:** Utilizing the space to create multiple access points and, during instruction, presentation opportunities.	**PRACTICES** 1. **Learners exhibit empathy with and tolerance for diverse ideas by:** Forming shared norms, engaging respectfully in vulnerable discussions, and working toward fostering trust and sharing when uncomfortable. 2. **School librarians facilitate experiences in which learners exhibit empathy and tolerance for diverse ideas by:** Sharing new, culturally relevant theory with peers through publications, articles, and podcasts to enhance the scope of classroom assignments and discussion.	**PRACTICES** 1. **Learners work productively with others to solve problems by:** Engaging in shared norms and respect agreements when receiving and providing constructive feedback. 2. **School librarians promote working productively with others to solve problems by:** Effectively monitoring and responding to breaches of shared norms and respect agreements in the school library space and during instruction.
C. SHARE	**ACTIVITIES** 1. Provide learners with the expectation and agency of discussing their chosen sources to encourage more authentic information-gathering practices. Highlight learners' selection patterns to invite deeper discussion about them. 2. Center learner voice by offering learners more options when presenting—for example, digital presentations, gallery walks around the school library space, short video clip reviews, and small-group experiences.	**ACTIVITIES** 1. Invite learners to use the school library space to share their stories and voices through moderated forums or open mic experiences. 2. Engage in learning and professional communities, subscribe to newsletters, and attend webinars to expand your knowledge base with relevant information and resources.	**ACTIVITIES** 1. Encourage learners to engage in their topic of interest by inviting them to create library materials, like booklists, displays, opinion pieces, and signage. 2. Prepare talking points, resources, or policies to assist in responding to breaches of shared norms and respect agreements so that response to behavior/language is quick, thoughtful, and effective.

	IV. CURATE	V. EXPLORE	VI. ENGAGE
C. SHARE	**PRACTICES** **1. Learners exchange information resources within and beyond their learning community by:** Actively engaging in and creating information sites using emerging technologies and sharing sites through social media channels. **2. The school library facilitates the contribution and exchange of information within and among learning communities by:** Modeling the necessity of ongoing collection evaluations and updates.	**PRACTICES** **1. School librarians prepare learners to engage with the learning community by:** Expanding your learning network to maximize access to materials and to grow professionally. **2. The school library prepares learners to engage with a larger learning community by:** Inviting specific community members and business owners to join some classes or programs via digital meeting software to establish real-world connections or introduce oral history into the classroom.	**PRACTICES** **1. School librarians promote the responsible, ethical, and legal sharing of new information with a global community by:** Encouraging responsibility and a critical mindset through sharing relevant examples and relevant consequences of unethical and irresponsible information consumption and reproduction. **2. The school library encourages participation in a diverse learning community to create and share information by:** Taking the school library on the go to collaborate with and assist educators and learners during lessons, providing supplemental materials and resources.
C. SHARE	**ACTIVITIES** 1. Share information sites with educators and learners of other learning communities to instill ethical responsibility for site contributions. Inspire and encourage curriculum expansion, supplementation, and development with their input. 2. Practice transparency with learners regarding the school library collection. Such openness offers opportunities to gather book suggestions and even analyze some titles through a responsive lens.	**ACTIVITIES** 1. Use digital meeting software to host/participate in casual, standing, monthly/bimonthly/quarterly town and school district librarian meetings. 2. Utilize digital meeting software and meeting recordings to become a member of a local chapter or learning community.	**ACTIVITIES** 1. Lend information services to school-wide groups that are representative of specific identities, such as affinity groups, to support their needs and help in their advocacy efforts with informed, credible, and valid information. 2. Facilitate digital discussion boards to act as moderated forums for learners to share information and remix ideas freely.

(cont'd)

FIGURE O.3

AASL Standards Frameworks applied to culturally responsive practice (cont'd)

	I. INQUIRE	II. INCLUDE	III. COLLABORATE
D. GROW	**PRACTICES** 1. **Learners participate in an ongoing inquiry-based process by:** Using the introspective exercise in Think when approaching future research. 2. **School librarians implement and model an inquiry-based process by:** Gathering insight from learners' feedback practices and behavior toward each other to improve instruction, learner/educator connection, and reflective methods.	**PRACTICES** 1. **School librarians explicitly lead learners to demonstrate empathy and equity in knowledge building within the global learning community by:** Appreciating the unique cultural understanding that each learner brings to assignments/exercises and modifying accordingly. 2. **The school library builds empathy and equity within the global learning community by:** Gathering insights about learner and family structure/communication methods through observation, conferences, and surveys.	**PRACTICES** 1. **School librarians foster active participation in learning situations by:** Promoting collaborative opportunities with educators and administrators through professional district networks and school library newsletters to increase visibility and impact. 2. **The school library supports active learner participation by:** Identifying and understanding the digital divide in the community, and growing the access network between the community and the school building.
D. GROW	**ACTIVITIES** 1. Create end-of-lesson reflection pieces that circle back to the pre-research thought exercise and encourage learners to follow this process before and after research projects to further affirm and challenge their personal values. 2. Empower yourself and other school librarians to continue learning about learners' values and viewpoints by sharing and reviewing new resources.	**ACTIVITIES** 1. Invite learners to evaluate the school library space and challenge accessibility to improve services, instruction, and layout. 2. Communicate with educators regularly to gain insight on different effective communication methods to extend reach and encourage involvement from reluctant learners and families.	**ACTIVITIES** 1. Model group work for learners to show the essential collaboration skills expected in global and technological society by regularly creating real-life scenarios within school library instruction. 2. Expand learners' and classroom educators' awareness of public libraries and local institutions to increase access to technology.

	IV. CURATE	V. EXPLORE	VI. ENGAGE
D. GROW	**PRACTICES** 1. **Learners select and organize information for a variety of audiences by:** Engaging with peers and school librarians to amplify learner voice in the school library space, collection, and resources. 2. **The school library engages the learning community in exploring resources by:** Instilling a sense of responsible use of school library space and resources through scheduling practices, 24/7 access to digital materials, and input via reviews and shared information sites.	**PRACTICES** 1. **School librarians help learners develop through experience and reflection by:** Using the introspective exercise in Think to improve, adapt, and modify your instructional mindset and including personal growth in your yearly goals. 2. **The school library assists in the growth and development of learners by:** Using the reflective exercise in Think to solidify the role of safety, bravery, inclusivity, and intellectual challenge in the school library space in a way that is evident to learners, educators, administrators, and stakeholders.	**PRACTICES** 1. **Learners engage with information to extend personal learning by:** Understanding previous behaviors regarding information ethics and participating in ongoing reflection when consuming and reproducing information. 2. **School librarians support learners' engagement with information to extend personal learning by:** Maintaining and regularly evaluating the school library collection to highlight the school librarian's dedication to accuracy and relevance.
D. GROW	**ACTIVITIES** 1. Encourage learners to take part in regular meetings, advisory committees, and feedback opportunities to foster responsible use and enhance an authentic culture of school library use. 2. Analyze school library–provided print and digital resource subscription usage to gain insight on relevance, awareness, and need.	**ACTIVITIES** 1. Creating an atmosphere of mutual respect and sharing takes time, as does developing cultural competency. Setting this type of work as a goal for your yearly professional development evaluations will allow for intentionally allotted, dedicated time. 2. Engage in subtle library space signage changes, collection audits, culturally relevant display themes, visible call-and-response activities, and learner surveys to model lifetime learning.	**ACTIVITIES** 1. Engage in learner reflection practices to better understand learners' positions versus the initial data gathered in Think. 2. Invite exposure to culturally responsive perspectives, booklists, materials, and research and curriculum guides via your personal learning networks or webinars.

PART I

School Librarian

Looking Inward

A s we walk the path toward cultural proficiency, reflective practices will become a cornerstone to lean into, rely on, and circle back on constantly. Self-reflection is a vital exercise in our profession. Establishing a better understanding of how we interact with and provide for learners, their families, and communities and how our experiences play into those moments invites growth, in ourselves and in our school libraries. Before we build culturally responsive school libraries, we need to do some work within ourselves through reflection, vulnerability, and honesty. The "inside-out" work, as Hammond (2015) wrote in *Culturally Responsive Teaching and the Brain*, involves "developing the right mindset, engaging in self-reflection, checking our implicit biases, practicing social-emotional awareness, and holding an inquiry stand regarding the impact of our interactions on students." By following the philosophies of the scholars mentioned in the introduction and Hammond's inside-out work, we will explore culture, identity, and bias as they relate to yourself, your space, and the learners you interact with.

Setting the Tone for Meaningful Conversations

Before diving into conversations about culture and identity, which naturally involve race, bias, and injustice, it is important that we (and in the future, those you practice with and instruct) are on the same page. Regardless of our individual belief systems, there are fundamental aspects of the discussions, examples, strategies, activities, and exercises that require a shared understanding. This shared understanding is formed by the collaborative creation of "norms" (figure 0.3, II.C.P1). Norms are a shared set of expectations that encourage safety in sensitive conversations. Inviting

3

vulnerability in discussions and situations that were previously sterile of emotion requires bravery—in all members. Sometimes, norms can help facilitate productive conversations that avoid common pitfalls like interruptions, distractions, personal attacks, assumptions, and power structures. Norms allow members of the discussion or situation to fall back on "rules" and expectations as a group to safeguard and empower their individual voices.

Creating norms should be a collaborative process. This is a great activity to introduce in your school library, whether you are creating expectations for the space or creating discussion protocols for collaborative instruction. You can include learners' voices through informal polls, candid group discussions, or thoughtful reflective prompts. By sharing in the creation of norms, learners are gaining authority over the school library space or instruction time. Learners will realize that their voices matter within the space, and this realization will translate into greater engagement with and shared responsibility for the materials. Let's start by introducing some norms into this process. The following norms, created by Nuri-Robins et al. (2012) in *Culturally Proficient Instruction: A Guide for People Who Teach*, translate well for our shared journey:

1. Be open to new insights.
2. Be willing to be surprised.
3. Accept that you will not always be right.
4. Understand that some of your closely held values may conflict with the values of cultural proficiency.
5. Remember that the goal of reading the book is not to complete it; the goal is to use the book to direct your thinking and your work as you engage in the lifelong process of becoming culturally proficient.

When translating the process of norm creation into the school library space, you can take several avenues. Some norms are better suited for an instructional setting, whereas other norms are more suited for setting the tone of the school library space. Similar to setting rules or boundaries with learners, establishing norms will set a tone and give you quick guidelines to fall back on. It is good to remember that creating norms should be a shared experience. If you choose to set these norms without learner input, make sure that you take time to survey learners or collaborate with them to modify the norms as needed.

NORMS IN OUR SPACES

Examples of Norms during Instruction

1. Lean into discomfort.
2. Listen actively.
3. Invite questions.
4. Practice patience.
5. Value individual truths.
6. Accept that you will not always be right.
7. Pause before reacting and responding.

Examples of Norms within the School Library Space

1. Respect others—their similarities and differences.
2. Treat the space and resources with respect—leave the space how you found it.
3. Follow behavioral and safety policies—if you would like a copy of the policy, please ask the school librarian.
4. Hate speech is not welcome—treat others with an inclusive and open mind.

The collaborative process of norm creation invites deeper conversations. Whether these conversations occur casually or formally, aloud or in writing, they should provide an authentic engagement opportunity to be culturally responsive. Respect and safety are experienced and understood differently by each individual. Your perception of what "respect" means and of what "safety" means in the school library setting will affect the language and directness of the policy you create. Sharing your perspectives with learners and hearing their definitions of those words will provide you insight that should invite intentional modifications to norms and policies for the school library space (figure 0.3, I.A.P2). Learning how the learners understand and experience respect and safety is vital to better understanding their position in the world and the ways in which this social-emotional awareness can present itself in the school library space.

As you build trust and introduce the creation of collaborative norms, mindful discussions about learner identity can take place. Asking learners to share their identities may involve inviting feelings of vulnerability or discomfort into the library space. By creating norms for your space, you safeguard learners and yourself from feeling emotionally drained, exposed, or targeted (figure 0.3, I.A.A2). With the shared set of norms as your base, you can form discussion protocols, such as limiting interruptions, judgment, and disruption, that facilitate and foster participation and cooperation.

CHALLENGE: CREATING NORMS

» What are some norms you would have included when beginning our shared journey?

» What are some norms that you can introduce into your school library space and during instruction?

» How would you invite learners' voices into this process?

» What is your understanding of and experience with respect and safety?

» Can you identify areas in which your understanding and experiences influence your work?

Exploring Your Identities

According to Hammond (2015, 53), "before you can leverage diversity as an asset in the classroom, you must reflect on the challenges that can interfere with open acceptance of students who are different from you in background, race, class, language, or gender." Challenges like bias, implicit or otherwise, can negatively impact our interactions with learners in a sometimes insidious way. By exploring and reflecting on our own identities and understanding our implicit biases, we can begin to work intentionally to dismantle those ideas and move forward on our journey toward cultural proficiency. First, let's work through the following activities to empower us to reflect deeply on our social and personal identities (figure 0.3, V.A.P1).

Social Identity Garden

Approach this activity as you would planting a garden. Each identity marker in your social identity garden is a plot that grows with attention and nourishment. Fill in the circles with your individual social identity markers (see figure 1.1 for an example). Most social identity markers are visible to others, but try to focus more on how you perceive yourself when completing this task. Give yourself time to work through each circle. You may find that you can fill in all of them or just a few. These identity markers are always evolving, so pause and reflect on where each of them fits into your life at the moment. You will find a blank Social Identity Garden Worksheet in appendix A.

FIGURE 1.1

Social identity garden example

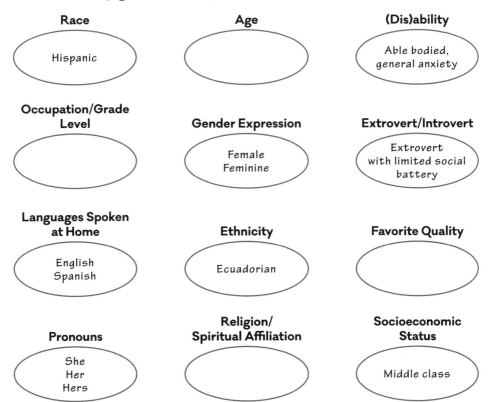

Race

Hispanic

Age

(Dis)ability

Able bodied, general anxiety

Occupation/Grade Level

Gender Expression

Female Feminine

Extrovert/Introvert

Extrovert with limited social battery

Languages Spoken at Home

English Spanish

Ethnicity

Ecuadorian

Favorite Quality

Pronouns

She Her Hers

Religion/ Spiritual Affiliation

Socioeconomic Status

Middle class

CHALLENGE: TENDING YOUR SOCIAL GARDEN

After you fill out the social identity garden with your individual identity markers, reflect on the following questions:

- » Which identity circles were the easiest to fill?
- » Which identity circles were the hardest to fill?
- » Which identity circles do you share or present when you are at work?
- » Which identity circles do you hide or not talk about when you are at work?
- » Which identity circles are you not able to hide?
- » Which identity circles are you never asked about at school?
- » Which identity circles do you consider essential to building relationships with your friends, your family members, or learners?

Personal Identity Garden

The second garden is your personal identity garden. This garden is full of personal interests. As in the social identity garden, each personal identity marker is a plot that grows with attention and nourishment. Fill in the circles with your individual personal identities (see figure 1.2 for an example). Most personal identity markers are less apparent to others, so this exercise is more about your interests and reflecting on those interests. Give yourself time to work through each circle. You may find that you can fill in all of them or just a few. These identity markers are always evolving, so pause and reflect on where each of them fits into your life at the moment. You will find a blank Personal Identity Garden Worksheet in appendix B.

FIGURE 1.2

Personal identity garden example

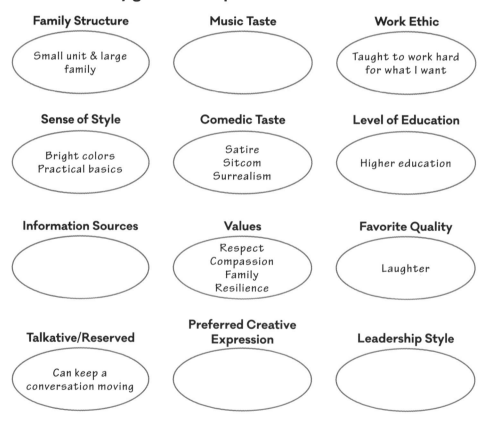

CHALLENGE: TENDING YOUR PERSONAL GARDEN

After you fill out the personal identity garden with your individual identity markers, reflect on the following questions:
» Which identity circles were the easiest to fill?
» Which identity circles were the hardest to fill?
» Which identity circles do you share or present when you are at work?
» Which identity circles do you hide or not talk about when you are at work?
» What makes those specific identity circles uncomfortable to share?
» Which identity circles are you never asked about at school?
» Which identity circles do you consider essential to building relationships with your friends, your family members, or learners?

Using identity gardens with learners at the start of a new year, at midyear, or whenever you start your journey will provide you a well-rounded look at each learner. The information gathered from this activity can help modify lessons, influence resources selected, and even help facilitate parent communications.

Your School Library, Your Self

Participating in reflective practices, such as the identity gardens, will highlight a number of different aspects of the self. There is the *self that we know*, the *self that is perceived by others*, and the *self that lives unconsciously within us*. The *self that we know* is based on traits both visible and invisible to others. It is based on the identity markers we perceive as part of our personality. We are still the *self that we know* as identity markers change over time, and we will continue to be our genuine selves as long as we feel grounded in our identities. It is important, however, to recognize the many identities we have at this very moment and realize that who we are influences what we do. Embracing a holistic approach, like this one, allows us to see ourselves as a combination of many identities and experiences—past, present, and future. The same approach is valuable when we turn our attention to empowering learners to explore their whole selves through reflective exercises. Their many identity markers will amplify our need to be proactive and responsive with our collections, lessons, and services.

When we reflect on the markers that differentiate one individual from the other, many important factors come to light. We experience varying gazes on our physical selves daily, leading to the formation of the *self that is perceived by others*. Some physical identity markers are inherently visible and perceived, positively and negatively, by others, while other markers go unnoticed or are easily concealed. Race and gender, for example, are aspects that can be readily discerned in some individuals and thus create an immediate advantage or disadvantage depending on their surroundings. Societal structures and ideals are systematically upheld, fostering the perpetration of bias and prejudice toward some identity markers versus others.

When individuals are unable to conceal the identity markers that are systematically opposed, they are at an immediate disadvantage and are marginalized from the approved dominant societal culture. Sometimes, when identity markers are less visible and not taken into account, in the case of racial, gender, and neurodivergent passing, the effects can be confusing to the individual's sense of self. When passing occurs, our identities begin to clash. As defined by Brown (1991), passing is

> an adaptation to circumstances of oppression . . . wherein individual members of various minority/subordinate groups will achieve an identity as a member of a dominant/superordinate group. . . . Any person with a stigmatizing attribute which is not apparent and who interacts with others without it being known is, to some extent, engaged in passing. (quoted in Kanuha 1999, 27–28)

Although passing occurs as a protective step toward assimilation, it is also fair to say that it can create tension in an individual's identity, thus masking their experiences with that identity.

Reflecting on dominant societal cultures in our country within the categories of race, abilities, gender, and sexual preference, among others, provides an opportunity to discuss the *self that lives unconsciously within us*. This self has been bombarded with messaging that emphasizes stereotypical representation and underrepresentation of differing races and stringent gender roles, stigmatizing various identities and other misrepresentations for years. These messages live in our minds, on the television series we watch, in the advertisements we see, in the conversations we are part of, in our ethnic or racial customs, and in the media we consume. These messages can influence the *self that lives unconsciously within us* because they work on a subconscious level. The frequency with which we see and are shown dominant societal culture makes it so that anything we see that does not fit those ideas seems foreign and out of place. It is nearly impossible to avoid the messages because they are part of our daily lives. Instead, culturally responsive practices encourage us to register the information we are absorbing passively and actively, recognize biased messages, and then analyze the situations in which we can intentionally bring inclusivity into our school libraries in order to intentionally grow and do better.

Understanding our biases, both implicit and explicit, is essential, especially because bias is inescapable. Every person experiences each minute of their life through a different lens. The lens is fortified by their personal outlook, values, and beliefs and by all their past experiences. Sometimes lenses are tinted with family experiences, values, and beliefs, which add layers to our own perspective. Other times lenses are obscured by prejudice and racist beliefs that need to be acknowledged and combatted. Exploring the layers of our lenses will allow us to understand how traits and beliefs like those in our identity gardens can influence our instruction, resource selection, decorations, expectations, communication, policies, and other aspects within the school library.

Cultural Memberships

In their book *Cultural Proficiency: A Manual for School Leaders*, Lindsey et al. (2019, 29) defined culture as "everything you believe and everything you do that enables you to identify with people who are like you and that distinguishes you from people who differ from you." The authors continued: "A culture is a group of people identified by their shared history, beliefs, values, and patterns of behavior" (29). The intersection between identity and culture exists because our identity markers can assist or deter us from becoming part of cultural groups. As explored in the introduction to this book, culture has many levels (Hammond 2015) and offers an opportunity to become part of a collective. Reflecting on the cultural memberships we hold—for example, our professional field's shared culture or our social cultures based on common interests—will help us better understand not only the many identities we present throughout the day but also the types of cultural nuances we navigate as a result.

For example, if we are reflecting on cultural membership as it relates to the school library, we should think of the many nonverbal and assumed ideals presented daily. Learners who are recent arrivals to the United States of America may not understand the basics of library use because they did not belong to or have the opportunity to belong to the cultural membership of library use. Though we could readily assume that learners, especially in the higher grade levels, understand the basics of library use, learners who have never used a library before could be hesitant to grab books off the shelves out of fear that they will be reprimanded. They could also be unaware that they can borrow books to take home, making the library experience counterproductive. By acknowledging the difference in understanding between cultural memberships, we can better equip the school library space to prevent confusion, intimidation, hesitations, unintentional exclusionary practices, and bias.

Using Reflection to Guide Your Journey

When you are lost, when you find yourself without support, when it feels like trying something new is not worth it, lean on reflective practices to guide your next move along the journey. Engaging in "inside-out work" (Hammond 2015) is a valuable way to take stock of where you are in the current moment. You will be able to assess your values, beliefs, and interests and better understand how those markers influence aspects of your work. As we move toward removing service barriers and establishing culture in instructional practices, it is important that we understand which lenses we peer through. The unconscious motivations, implicit bias, and dominant societal ideals that live within us will not be ignored. Instead we will work to acknowledge them and use antibias and culturally responsive practices to bring forth intentional change.

Mindful Modeling

Putting our inward reflections into action through modeling is the natural next step in this journey. We can begin to incorporate new perspectives into our spaces and practice, with patience and flexibility in mind. We, as school librarians, are in a position of power; we manage our collections, spaces, and learners, but we do not always get the credit we deserve. Our work is not always understood or appreciated. Implementing culturally responsive practices is a way to equip ourselves with a boat off our librarian island and reinforce our relationships with mainlanders in a way that validates our work and our impact on learner experience. In a more positive vein, however, we can use our position of power to make a difference. For example, we have the ability through our book selection and instructional exercises to raise consciousness about prominent figures and events that are not usually in the limelight because they fall outside the societal norm or are perceived as belonging to a marginalized community. Using our position to positively influence others through culturally responsive work begins with small steps that culminate in a substantial impact.

Leading Learners

It is an inevitable truth that we bring ourselves into our profession. As we travel this path of cultural responsiveness, we will be reflecting on just about everything we do in our school libraries. We will be working inward to influence our outward actions. To encourage growth in our spaces, ourselves, and our learners, we should take opportunities to try new methods and invite vulnerability into our practice. Inviting vulnerability by discussing norms, shared and differing cultural reference viewpoints on respect, authority, praise/shame, and collaboration, and our trial and error and common missteps when researching allows us to build a trusting exploratory environment and connect with learners on a personal level.

Our learning environment will encourage learners and other educators to engage in their topics of interest and to identify and reflect on viewpoints that affirm and challenge their personal perspectives and preconceived notions, while honoring their frame of reference. To do that, we will place value in the unique understanding that each learner brings to each assignment, exercise, activity, and program by displaying reflective practices and by providing authentic discussion opportunities and shared learning experiences. Many of these experiences will come from instruction, where we can show learners how to intentionally reflect, discuss civilly, and consume information responsibly. We can model those experiences using the strategies along our journey as appropriate for our learners and our school community. We can combine our lessons for ethical use of information and responsible information gathering with an informed perspective on censorship and ethics. The discussion of censorship will naturally include topics that involve vulnerability and the need to rely on the discussion/space norms created early in the culturally responsive journey (figure 0.3, VI.A.P1).

Creating or fostering an already existing atmosphere in which learners feel empowered and interactions are initiated is possible through engagement and ownership. Making our school libraries more relevant includes giving learners a voice and modeling the type of atmosphere we want to nurture. For example, inviting learners to use their creativity to produce school library materials such as booklists, displays, opinion pieces, and signage not only highlights their interests and passions but also gives us the opportunity to take a step back and allow others to have a creative say over the school library space (figure 0.3, III.C.A1). If you have a strong relationship with learners and have already created book clubs or socially engaging library clubs, try encouraging learners to take part in groups that can create positive change in the school library as well. Groups like advisory committees can take on survey creation, policy analysis, or translations of printed and digital materials or provide valued feedback on school library services based on their shared and individual experiences (figure 0.3, II.A.A2). Learners will gain a sense of ownership, which will enhance the culture of library use in the overall school community. They will be more likely to become advocates for the school library, and their trust will ensure that we return the favor.

Dedicated Digital Space

Nurturing a culturally responsive school library space entails focusing outward by modeling what we want learners and other educators to inhabit and maintain. The same concept applies to digital spaces. If we are supplementing our practices with digital services, we want to ensure that we understand and translate the culturally responsive and inclusive school library we are building in person. With the increasing need to provide digital services and resources, it is vital to continue our culturally responsive and inclusive stance within those areas. We can do this by analyzing digital resource subscription services and e-book collections. Analyzing data points provided by the subscription services will show us how many people are using the services and give us an idea of how to better advertise them (figure 0.3, IV.D.A2). By diving deeper into our digital resources with a culturally responsive lens, we can gain valuable insights about whether the resources provide a relevant assortment of information to fit the needs of our learners and our fellow educators. Analyzing digital reading collections is just as important. Just as we will look at our physical collections through a critical lens, we should do so with our digital collections. All reading materials, whether in person or digital, deserve our attention, especially if we want those materials to be relevant to our learners and to provide worldly experiences and credible information (figure 0.3, V.B.P2).

Using the same approach with technology within the school library can also provide valued insight. By conducting a simplified technology needs assessment of the school library highlighting points of concern, learner needs, and service gaps, our digital services and equipment offerings can stay on track technologically (figure 0.3, VI.A.A2). A technology needs assessment will provide you an outline of possible improvements within the space regarding the services already available. Although most technological upgrades are out of our control, this type of exercise can prioritize potential problem areas, so that we can propose strategic equipment upgrades, apply for grants, and appeal to those in power with reason on our side. For those on the other side of the budget spectrum, using the school library budget to purchase practical gadgets, tablets, and maker technology is a valid way to increase access to technology for learners who may not have access to those devices at home. It is impossible to predict what learners will need socially, emotionally, or educationally speaking, but anticipating their needs with careful surveys and room observations can improve our school library spaces' impact and relevance in the school community (figure 0.3, VI.A.P2).

Collaborating Creatively

As we continue the journey and learn more about culturally responsive practices, we must continue to be intentional with our actions and ask more of our learners and fellow educators. Asking more from our learners or fellow educators does not translate to asking favors or taking time out of their instruction; it is more about an emotional investment. Part of culturally responsive practices is learning from others and valuing their life experiences. Along our journey to make our selections, programs, instruction, and spaces more culturally responsive, we will constantly try to collaborate with others and highlight the relevancy of our school libraries—"try" being the operative word. From personal experience, being a school librarian can, at times, feel like being a door-to-door salesperson. Incorporated in our many varied duties is the need to sell our services to other educators and administrators with an almost survivalist instinct.

If schedules align and technology cooperates, we can foster valued partnerships and provide learners with an abundance of valuable resources. At the start, collaboration may look like a shared online document with out-of-the-box credible sources updated continuously to expose other educators and learners to areas of interest and advocacy (figure 0.3, I.B.A2). Online documents are great ways to share resources as evolving lists for fellow educators and learners to access and share easily. Creating documents or utilizing an online platform to share resources, either as a list or divided by content area, is a terrific way to increase visibility and impact while encouraging collaborative opportunities with other educators and administrators. Sharing information sites with fellow educators of other learning communities or content areas can encourage participation in the form of responsible resource sharing and encourage curriculum expansion, creative supplementation of lessons, and development from authentic classroom educator involvement (figure 0.3, IV.C.A1). Instilling a sense of ownership of school library space and resources through 24/7 access to digital materials and contribution via shared information sites or programs is a valuable task to take on. With collaboration comes conversation. Fellow educators can share valuable information regarding insight on different effective communication methods to reach learners and families, which will lead to more relevant and informed publicity efforts to extend reach and invite community involvement.

Collaboration may also look like class visits scheduled within the school library space, during which we read to learners, provide instruction regarding digital research databases, or curate materials for independent reading lessons. Aside from traditional collaboration opportunities, we can also lend information services to school-wide groups that are representative of a specific identity, called affinity groups, to cater to their specific needs and help in their advocacy efforts with informed, credible, and valid information (figure 0.3, VI.C.A1). Groups like the Asian American Heritage Club, Black Student Union, or Genders & Sexualities Alliance, or groups that cater to a specific interest like the Anime Club or Drama Club, provide us an opportunity to not only meet learners where they are comfortable but also offer a friendly face that they can associate with the school library. Affinity or interest groups offer great insight into cultural identities and social identities that can influence school library services. As with most outreach, approaching groups and attending their meetings before sharing entertaining and informational resources requires a blend of listening to the needs of the groups' learners and keeping an open mind.

Outside the school building, collaborative efforts are ruled by availability. Of course, in an ideal world, there would be time for everything including attending committee meetings and contributing to state-wide projects or presentations. Unfortunately, time is not always on our side. Fortunately, however, by utilizing digital meeting software and meeting recordings, becoming a member of a local chapter or learning community is less time consuming than in previous years. Watching meeting recordings or flipping through conference presentations on digital platforms allows for an increased intentional learning opportunity. An example that has proven impactful to our district's school library culture is the use of digital meeting software to host and participate in casual, standing monthly/bimonthly/quarterly town and school district librarian meetings. Having these meetings allowed for a sense of unity among school libraries in the district and allowed us the opportunity to participate in a library-specific community where we can share and learn from each other (figure 0.3, V.C.A1).

The culturally responsive journey requires us to seek out information, challenge ourselves with new practices, and evolve as the practice evolves. There are many directions to go with the foundation of culturally responsive and inclusive practices. Exploring anti-racist and antibias practices, for example, is a way to bring forth action and intentional change while building upon the work we are learning on this journey. We can continue to learn by staying in tune with the rest of the profession, reading about issues and injustice, and participating in a shared learning environment via digital platforms, meetings, and presentations (figure 0.3, V.C.P1).

Proactive School Library Policy

Policies give us a leg to stand on during times of friction and disagreement. They are also usually indicative of the population served, which should make them an example of culturally responsive work. As learners' needs evolve and populations change, policies must be revisited to appropriately reflect their needs. Our school libraries are sometimes forgotten in school policy creation, so it is up to us to research, write, and propose a new policy that specifically addresses the needs of the school library space and its learners. It is vital that we safeguard not only our communal areas, the learning environment, and collections but also ourselves. With book challenges and legislative actions looming over many states, policy should provide a way to ensure that appropriate and approved procedure is considered.

Although not all of us have the authority to create policy or make policy changes for the school library, we all have a new mindset and strategies with which to analyze the existing policy enacted for our school libraries (figure 0.3, II.A.P1). If you do not have authority from your school board or principal to create a new or change the existing school library policy, start with analyzing the existing policy through a culturally responsive lens. Print or save a digital copy, and start writing on it with intention. Note points of contention, add policy points and supporting viewpoints, and garner support from learners and fellow educators. Include a small group of learners and chosen educators in the evaluation process, increasing agency in the school library space (figure 0.3, II.A.A2). Agency will lead to advocacy, which is vital when proposing changes to the school board or administration. Presenting researched adjustments and learner/educator-led perspectives can lead to a more solid stance against naysayers.

If you have authority over school library policy creation and modification, there are a few areas in which to start an audit. Possible starting points include analyzing school population data and identifying unnecessary barriers to access and unclear language. School population data via the Common Core of Data are readily available online for public schools and private schools from the National Center for Education Statistics (figure 0.3, II.A.A1). The data include school directory information, school details, and enrollment characteristics. With these data, we gain information about the number of learners in "each grade level," "enrollment by race/ethnicity," "enrollment by gender," and the number of learners who are "free lunch eligible," "reduced-price lunch eligible," and "directly certified." Although the data collected are classified into limited categories of race and gender, they give us insight into some of our learners' financial situations and an idea of their cultural backgrounds as a school population. Having access to this information can influence our collections, programs, language use, and policy. For example, if our collections and signage do not mirror the cultural experiences and needs of our learners and their families, then we can work toward improving those areas within our spaces. Given some idea of the financial needs of our learners and their families, we can adjust our policies accordingly. If we have a circulation limit or late fee with a population that would benefit from open access and a fine-free structure, changes to policy can bring forth positive impact. We should use these evaluation opportunities to remove unnecessary barriers to access for all current and future learners and educators.

Identifying unnecessary barriers to access and unclear language is another important step in evaluating school library policy. Unnecessary barriers to access include fees, circulation limits, space use limitations, and any other policy points that discourage or deter learners from accessing resources. Although we can perform an initial evaluation of existing policies by ourselves, true insight will come from including others in the process (figure 0.3, III.B.P2). Using this process as an opportunity to include learner and educator perspectives and experiences can seem daunting, but it can allow us to expand our reach and create equitable, responsive policy in our libraries. If you are worried about input overload, prompt your small focus group with limited sections of the school library policy. A possible place to start is by asking learners and other educators for their input regarding their school library experiences and how they interact with the power structures in the space. Safeguarding our learners, ourselves, and our school libraries with approved policy is essential for promoting engagement and ensuring growth of the program. The American Library Association (ALA) provides talking points, strategies, and procedures that can protect materials and resources from content challenges (figure 0.3, IV.B.A1).

Yearly Plans for Attainable Goals

Creating an atmosphere of mutual respect and sharing takes time. More likely than not, time is not always on our side. The improvements and mindful changes we want to make require a sense of intention and understanding. Although there is no guarantee that there will be time to set every exercise, activity, project, and strategy into motion, we must attempt to dedicate some time for them to prove meaningful and impactful. Learning about identity, cultures, bias, race, injustice, privilege, equity, and inclusion is part of an endless journey. Actively engaging in and welcoming new concepts invites positive change to your practices and your school library.

At the start of the school year, we are encouraged to set goals for ourselves. Those goals are either part of our observation structure or simply attempts to improve our practice. Regardless of the reason or structure in mind, I encourage you to set culturally responsive school library services as a professional goal in the coming year. Setting culturally responsive practices as a goal for your yearly professional development plans will provide you dedicated time and purpose for continuing this journey (figure 0.3, V.D.A1). It will let your supervisors and administrators know that culturally responsive practice is a priority in your professional growth. As we continue this journey, set your intentions early and have confidence in the positive impact that will come from expanding your perspectives in your school library.

PART II

School Library

3

Working with What You Have

School libraries come in many forms. Depending on the school, they may be book sanctuaries, a hangout spot for learners during noninstructional time, technologically advanced media centers full of activity tubs and worktables, or a combination of each. Whether your school's library falls somewhere in between or drastically out of range, the opportunity to bring in culturally responsive principles exists. As we begin this journey, there are areas within the school library space that could transform quicker than others. There are ideas and activities that will take time to explore and implement but will ultimately change the look or feel of the school library space. Exploring new display themes, curating resources, and analyzing subsections of the collection will provide actionable steps and a thoughtful starting point (figure 0.3, VI.B.P2). With culturally responsive principles as a scaffold and with the framework to rely on, these actions will highlight the necessity of providing culturally responsive materials in the school library setting and what those materials may look like and will empower you to continue the journey.

Expanding Readers' Advisory Networks

Culturally responsive materials include stories that not only offer learners a look into their own culture but also expose them to the cultures of others. When I discuss materials, I am talking about the books on our shelves, the digital subscription services we maintain, the websites that we use to instruct learners, and the magazines that we have lying around or that exist digitally.

As the school library offers learners and other educators a wider array of materials to choose from, the requests start rolling in, and circulation increases. Whether you are an instructor or operate under a flexible schedule, I am sure that colleagues are picking your brain for reading material for their classrooms, their relatives, and their personal lives. School librarians are expected to have titles and websites in their back pocket, at hand when the information is needed. Luckily, there are culturally responsive resources that can take your suggestions to a new level.

The organization We Need Diverse Books offers a Pinterest board that houses culturally responsive read-alikes for a multitude of grade levels. Not only does this tool expand our readers' advisory skills and expose us to new titles, but it also offers the reader an explanation for why the second book is suggested. This tool and those like it can also be used when curriculums are being updated. Core texts that may be less culturally responsive can be supplemented or combined with a more relevant title. This approach is also helpful when supporting a colleague within their classroom. Offering a fellow educator who has taught the same couple of books for years a chance to explore the same theme with newer characters may offer a desired respite from the same old thing (figure 0.3, VI.D.A2). Other valued resources are found within the book awards circuit. Many book awards and grants highlight culturally inclusive titles. These awards lists can be nationwide, state-wide, regional, and even hyper-local. The lists can provide you a solid readers' advisory database to choose from and suggestions for the school library collection.

Display Themes and Thoughtful Selection

Book displays are a common practice in library work. We highlight our school library's collection by setting a theme and pulling a couple of books from the shelves. Depending on the time of year, the grade band, the new hit show, or a popular internet trend, these displays offer the school librarian a creative opportunity to draw in learners (figure 0.3, V.B.P2). When showcasing books, the school librarian holds the power. We get to choose the theme, select which books we will be setting aside, and decide where in our spaces this creative piece will live. Often, it is easiest to put together a display when we are knowledgeable about the theme. We pull from what we know and expand on our choices based on the space we have.

CHALLENGE:
CULTURALLY RESPONSIVE BOOK DISPLAYS

Pause to challenge yourself for a moment. For every book display that comes to mind when you are reading this chapter, think about the books that you normally highlight.

» Are you including stories or themes about people of color?
» How about authentic characters of color?
» If there are characters who are people of color, are there positive storylines that aren't drenched in tragedy?
» Are there characters presented who are differently abled?
» Are there characters who are of varied gender identities or sexual orientations?

If the answers to these questions are leaning toward no, then there is work to be done.

Providing culturally responsive materials in visible ways allows learners the ability to explore serious topics in a safe, controlled environment without feeling like they are fighting a stigma. As Bucher and Hinton (2013, 10) stated,

> in addition to helping students develop reading, writing, speaking, and listening skills, [young adult literature] can offer a connection to alienated students, mirror the lives of young adults, improve literacy skills, and provide a forum for adolescents to discuss what it means to come of age, including navigating difficult problems, accessing tools needed to become problem solvers, and fostering empathy.

By exploring coming-of-age topics through the eyes of culturally inclusive characters, learners may feel empowered to discuss and work through potentially sensitive moments with peers or family or even within the school library space.

Buying, displaying, and embedding books into the school library space that include characters from racial and ethnic minorities, characters with disabilities, and characters who identify as LGBTQ written by authors who share their characters' identities shows that you are knowledgeable about the population you serve and are an advocate for all learners including the underrepresented voices. Movements like #DisruptTexts, #WeNeedDiverseBooks, and more paved the path for highlighting and increasing access to authentically written titles featuring a wide array of identities. Not every book in the school library will represent every population, but including characters whom learners can identify with is essential to increase engagement with the collection. There shouldn't be a checklist for the number of books we put on display in the school library based on representing this or that population. It is about being aware of the differences within each learner and highlighting the value of those differences through relevant texts. An important point to keep in mind is that none of the challenges, activities, or ideas included here are meant to shame you, your school library space, or any of the books or displays that were made. Whatever our displays may have looked like yesterday, they will continue to evolve daily. Our choices in the school library space are like the actions in the continuum of cultural proficiency. One day we may be in one place, one day in another, and sometimes in two places on the same day. We must push ourselves to embrace an environment of constant learning and inclusivity.

Book displays are an excellent opportunity to channel the culturally responsive principles discussed in the introduction. For example, let's focus on Gay's (2002) five characteristics of culturally responsive teaching. Within these characteristics lie the essential pieces of teaching learners to "know and praise their own and each other's cultural heritages" and incorporating "multicultural information, resources, and materials in all subjects and skills routinely taught in schools." If we expand the notions of "cultural heritage" and "multicultural(ism)" to include other facets of commonly marginalized populations, our net of discovery is wider, and more identities can be represented authentically in the books displayed. A strategy that has proven helpful is the inclusion of a yearly calendar that highlights widely recognized awareness months for different groups, cultures, and causes (figure 0.3, VI.B.A2). This calendar will allow you to access a plethora of events to make displays for.

There are days of the year that are set aside to celebrate differences in ability, like World Braille Day, and monthlong celebrations such as National Native American Heritage Month that celebrate cultural groups. These calendars are sometimes called Diversity Calendars, Multicultural Calendars, or Diversity and Inclusivity Calendars. A benefit in using a calendar (figure 3.1) and modifying as needed is that it acts like a planning document for the school library space. The themed displays can be planned in advance, supplemental materials can be gathered, and, if needed, approval can be granted well in advance.

Focusing on the Collection

Studying your school's population data will also give you a perspective on the cultural, socioeconomic, ability, and language needs of the learners who use your school library space. If you already have an idea of your school's population, start exploring those needs and think critically about the books that line the shelves. There is never enough time to focus on collection development properly, but taking a microscope to only one section may offer you fewer materials to work with and still have the desired effect.

FIGURE 3.1

Culturally responsive school library calendar

September

Library Card Sign-Up Month
Banned Books Week (Varies)
Sept. 5–11 | National Suicide Prevention Week
Sept. 11 | Patriot Day
Sept. 15–Oct. 15 | Latinx/Hispanic Heritage Month

November

Native American Heritage Month
Trans Awareness Month
Picture Book Month
Media Literacy Week (Varies)
Nov. 11 | Veterans Day
Nov. 13–19 | Transgender Awareness Week
Nov. 25 | Thanksgiving Day
Nov. 26 | Native American Heritage Day

January

National Braille Literacy Month
Jan. 18 | Martin Luther King Jr. Day
Jan. 17–21 | No Name-Calling Week
Jan. 27 | Holocaust Remembrance Day

March

Women's History Month
Read Across America
Mar. 1 | Zero Discrimination Day
Mar. 2 | Read Across America Day
Mar. 8 | International Women's Day
Mar. 21–25 | National LGBTQ Health Awareness Week

May

Asian Pacific American Heritage Month
Mental Health Month
May 30 | Memorial Day

July

Disability Pride Month
July 26 | Disability Independence Day
July 30 | International Day of Friendship

October

Sept. 15–Oct. 15 | Latinx/Hispanic Heritage Month
Islamic Heritage Month
LGBT History Month
Italian-American Heritage and Culture Month
National Bullying Prevention Month
Oct. 5 | World Teachers' Day
Oct. 10 | Indigenous Peoples' Day
Oct. 21 | International Pronouns Day

December

Dec. 1 | World Aids Day
Dec. 3 | International Day of Persons with Disabilities
Dec. 10 | Human Rights Day

February

Black History Month
National Library Lovers Month
Random Acts of Kindness Week (Varies)
World Read Aloud Day (Varies)
Feb. 3 | National Women and Girls in Sports Day

April

School Library Month
Autism Awareness Month
National Poetry Month
National Library Week (Varies)
Apr. 2 | World Autism Awareness Day
Apr. 22 | Earth Day

June

LGBTQ+ Pride Month
Immigrant Heritage Month
June 19 | Juneteenth

August

National Book Lovers Day (Varies)
Aug. 19 | World Humanitarian Day
Aug. 23 | International Day for the Remembrance of the Slave Trade and Its Abolition
Aug. 26 | Women's Equality Day

For example, my learners were increasingly asking for graphic novels written in Spanish. As a result, I analyzed my graphic novel collection. I saw that the collection was lacking, first in graphic novel options in general, but then more specifically in Spanish-language graphic novels. Seeing this as an opportunity to expand school library services, engage a new set of learners, and mold the collection based on learners' needs, I took action. My bulk orders are processed through Follett Destiny, whose website offers the ability to filter the search results by language, offers the age recommendation, and offers series sets when appropriate. There weren't many results, but it gave me a starting point. It also opened my eyes to the other Spanish-language titles available that may be useful as supplemental materials for classrooms, like graphic novel Spanish-language versions of *Pride and Prejudice.* This type of support, through the ordering interface, allowed me to fill the gap in the collection, based on the needs of the learners. I also turn to the learners who are more comfortable reading in Spanish to offer suggestions of stories of all kinds. This type of work can be done by making a passive form available in the school library space or by visiting language classes for insight. I focused on looking for Spanish-language fiction and nonfiction titles, but these strategies can be used for all language needs.

"Diversity audits" are also helpful when analyzing the collection, even if starting with a small subsection. Certain cataloging software, like Follett Destiny's TitleWave and Mackin, come equipped with a Diversity Audit function. The collection analysis capabilities highlight pertinent information about the entire collection, like publication dates, Dewey Decimal Classification system comparisons, incomplete records, number of items, and the age of the collection. Take these data and narrow the scope. Pick one subsection of the school library's collection. I recommend starting with a section like the 900s. I focused on the 900s and dug deep into the collection "by the tens." This strategy showed me the different subsections within the 900s section, which also correspond with the history of different parts of the world. The same can be done for the 800s section. Each of these sections houses materials from different places all over the world, and if your school library collection is anything like mine, those subsections will be underrepresented.

For example, I had hundreds of books in 940 History of Europe and 970 History of North America, but only about thirty books in 960 History of Africa and four books in 980 History of South America. Similar trends were found in the 800s section. If the school does not provide cataloging software that has collection analysis capabilities, a shelf read may just do the trick. Auditing the collection through a culturally responsive lens opens the door to student voice. If you have volunteers or aides, this approach could be an opportunity to involve them in the collection maintenance process (figure 0.3, IV.B.P1).

An excellent opportunity for learner involvement related to the school library collection is the formation of focus groups or advisory committees. Nurturing a small group of learners who care about their school library is difficult but worthwhile. Online surveys and other digital tools make it easier to survey learners and understand their relationship with and habits within the school library. Once learners' school library habits are better understood, relationships can be formed, and agency can begin. A focus group or advisory committee can lend their time to collection analysis projects and diversity audits using resources like *Reading Diversity: A Tool for Selecting Diverse Texts* from the Learning for Justice organization, formerly named Teaching Tolerance (figure 0.3, IV.B.A2).

Learning for Justice (2016) notes,

> Traditionally, tools that aid text selection have focused on quantitative and qualitative measures like complexity, word and sentence length, cohesion, language features, and knowledge demands. But these tools do *not* include diversity and representation, critical literacy, or reader and task as part of the selection criteria. *Reading Diversity* is different. This model promotes a multi-dimensional approach to text selection that prioritizes critical literacy, cultural responsiveness, *and* complexity. (italics in original)

With this tool, learners and other educators can survey a handful of books, with guided questions that relate to race, ethnicity, gender, class, age, ability, religion, place, immigration status, LGBTQ+ identities, and more. This tool might also be helpful when evaluating texts for stereotypes or misrepresentations. Learning for Justice offers not only this tool but also classroom resources, magazines and publications, professional development, and frameworks for instruction to support social justice work in education.

Small focus groups or advisory committees with committed members not only foster a sense of agency between the learners and the school library but also nurture critical thinking and advocacy efforts. The learners who take part in collection development can then go on to make displays, evaluate the space, analyze policy, and be an advocate for the school library when called upon. Including learners in essential pieces of the school library puzzle can cultivate a formative school library community.

Access across Platforms, Spaces, Abilities

Part of managing the collection is ensuring that the materials and resources can be accessed inside and outside the school building. Expanding access to materials and resources to learners outside the school building not only encourages and fosters literacy but also nurtures digital citizenship (figure 0.3, I.B.P2). Learners are familiar with having information available to them at the touch of a screen, but as we know, that ability results in an overwhelming amount of information that is not always credible. Although learners can access information through search practices and by wandering down rabbit holes, passively ingesting information without understanding strategies like bias, misinformation, disinformation, and propaganda can turn quick and easy information gathering into a possibly insidious task.

Guiding learners in the practice of responsible information gathering when they leave the school building can be facilitated by embracing digital technologies. Utilizing online educational portals, digital classroom spaces, and social media platforms can increase awareness of and engagement with the digital resources provided by the school library. It's impossible to control what and how learners access when they leave the school building, but increasing awareness of resources like databases, e-books, and guided research website lists should make learners' lives easier, which in turn may encourage them to value those services. The engagement struggle is a real one that isn't easily fixed. Exploring the different avenues by which learners ingest information can open up new service areas within your school library work.

An important aspect to keep in mind when talking about digital resources and accessibility is the exclusivity that exists in accessing the internet in some of our communities (figure 0.3, VI.A.P2). The digital divide is very real, and some of our learners fall victim to no/low/insufficient internet access in their living arrangements. With the recent emphasis due to necessity, the education world shifted into a digital sphere. As we school librarians rushed to make our resources available to homebound learners and educators, there was a push to use our profession, turn it upside down, and restructure our everyday practices to meet the needs of our schools. The emphasis on digital resources is always paired with the increased need for gadgets and barrier-free access points available to learners. A Pew Research Center analysis found that "some 15% of U.S. households with school-age children do not have a high-speed internet connection at home" (Anderson and Perrin 2018). Although this problem affects learners of all races and ethnicities, learners from Black and Hispanic households are most frequently affected. Familiarizing yourself with research about digital access and concerns about equitable access can benefit not only the learners affected but also other educators as they modify their lessons, assignments, and practices.

With regard to the collection, a better understanding of the limits that exist in your communities related to internet access or information-gathering habits will only improve the services you can share with and provide to learners and fellow educators (figure 0.3, III.D.P2). Although school libraries seldom have gadgets or internet access points for learners to borrow, public libraries and local institutions can act as extended shared spaces for learners to study, complete their homework, access necessary resources, and grow. Empowering learners, especially those in typically marginalized populations, by pointing them in the direction of community public services is a vital practice in fostering culturally responsive-sustaining school library spaces (figure 0.3, III.D.A2).

Intentional Actionable Steps

As a school librarian whose resources are scarce and whose days fly by in a blink, time is not always on your side. There are learners waiting to be taught, piles of books waiting to be processed, and daily tasks that get pushed regularly. With all the inescapable tasks funneled through the school library door, is it any wonder that time speeds by? With intentional actionable steps, the culturally responsive practices that you decide to implement in your school library space will be structured into feasible tasks. Each task is grounded in a specific purpose and can be expanded or modified as appropriate for your space. By expanding your readers' advisory networks, modifying displays, and analyzing the collection in smaller sections, you can work with the culturally responsive materials you have, work toward more responsive and inclusive displays, and engage learners authentically inside and outside the school library space.

4

Step into the Library

The school library is a nebulous environment. It is a mash-up of classroom, traditional library, computer lab, makerspace, social space, quiet retreat, and whatever else fits the school's needs. Most of all, school libraries have the ability to act as tangible representations of learners, the school community, and our individual styles as librarians. The many hours we spend in our spaces allow us the comfort of knowing the exactitudes of their layout and purpose but also create blind spots about natural patterns and necessary progress. Blind spots inhibit the services we provide, the types of programs and lessons we plan, and the emotional safety of those using the school library space. Although it is impossible to guard everyone's emotional well-being, it is our responsibility to make sure that the school library space doesn't add to any emotional turmoil because of our choices. Forcing ourselves to "walk a mile in someone else's shoes" can provide us new perspectives that can influence a reevaluation of our space and services.

Our Places in Society and the School Library

Reflecting on our introspective journey in chapter 1, we realize that there are aspects of our identities that are vital to who we are but that often go unseen. Our identities, as we learned, come with positive and negative perceptions, biases, and privileges. Most of the time, areas of our identity that lead to privilege are beyond our control. To have privilege means having an advantage over another person without merit or control. Usually, privilege goes unnoticed until the person with the advantage no longer has that advantage and must live outside dominant societal norms or structures. For example, if you are able-bodied and break your leg, you become aware of your mobility, the accessibility of your favorite spaces, expectations of behaviors like having the door opened for you, and circumstances that you never knew or expected to be an issue before. Those whose identities fall outside the dominant societal norm or structure are afforded fewer services, opportunities, or rights more often than not. Privilege is not something we can avoid or shed, but as we become self-aware, we can seize opportunities to learn from and use our privileged position to open doors for those who are disenfranchised.

Pause to challenge yourself for a moment. Reflection is the best first step when challenged with new ideas and terms. Think about the identity markers you pinpointed in chapter 1. Compare your identity markers with those that society considers dominant (also referred to as normal, acceptable, superior, crucial, etc.). Whether your identity falls inside, outside, or in between those societal norms considered dominant and nondominant, reflect on the nuanced or blatant advantages you've received and times at which you've experienced disenfranchisement and prejudice.

COMMON TYPES OF PRIVILEGE AND THE DOMINANT SOCIETAL NORM

- » Ability: Able-bodied is the dominant societal norm.
- » Age: The dominant societal norm can vary between youth and middle age in comparison to elderly.
- » Body size: "Standard sizes" are the dominant societal norm in comparison to "plus sizes."
- » Gender: Male is the dominant societal norm.
- » Geographical location: Western/American is the dominant societal norm.
- » Race: White/Caucasian is the dominant societal norm.
- » Religion: Christianity is the dominant societal norm.
- » Sexuality: Heterosexuality is the dominant societal norm.

Continually revisiting the reflective process is vital in this journey and can give you the opportunity to check in with your mindset before, during, and after culturally responsive exercises. Taking privilege into consideration, we can start to reevaluate the school library space thoughtfully. Although we cannot grasp the immensity of the positive and negative of other people's experiences, it is important to reflect on our own privileges and how we perpetuate dominant societal norms in the school library space. This reflection will shed light on areas within the space that are lacking because they fail to serve those in nondominant and overlooked societies.

Seeing the Space with New Eyes

Next time you enter your school library space, have the intention of viewing it through a critical lens. In this experiment, the word *critical* does not mean "negative" (figure 0.3, V.A.P2). Instead, think of this exercise as adding a lens to the personal lenses through which we see daily. Putting this critical lens in front of our personal lenses allows us to explore outside our preconceived notions and view the space from a new perspective. A great method for analyzing any space, program, event, or experience is to gather notes. Take notes and organize your findings into three categories: what you see, what it indicates/reveals, how it can improve.

Walk through your school library as if for the first time. Pretend someone else hung up the signs on the walls or set up the displays. Notice every sign, every art piece, and every poster. Take on the perspective of learners who are new to the school, who have different needs, who are native speakers of a language other than English, or who may not have experienced a library setting before. First, identify signs that have implied meaning or unclear language. Providing learners more direct expectations, directions, and guidance will minimize misunderstandings that stem from miscommunication. Clearing the space of vague and outdated signage will give us the opportunity to rethink the messages we want to convey in the school library space. For example, if a multitude of signs are taking up valuable display space and they all say the same thing or are irrelevant, then here is an opportunity to remove them and install one sign with concise wording that conveys the desired school library culture. The pared-down signage will not only highlight the rule but also provide space for displaying new posters, interactive exhibits, or artwork made by learners.

CHALLENGE: SIGNAGE

Start by superficially evaluating the signage in the school library. Focus on one sign at a time. Evaluate each for the following characteristics: quantity, quality, significance, relevance, inclusivity. Ask yourself the following:

» What is this sign saying?
» Is this sign's message implied or direct?
» What is the tone of this sign?
» What types of images and identities is this sign portraying, if any?
» Is this sign still relevant to the school library space and policies?
» What steps can I take to modify the signage for the better?

Sometimes we must create rules inside the school library space that are pseudo commonsense reminders to learners. I'm thinking of reminders like "please push in your seat," "no racing with the rolling chairs," or "no drinking/eating around the computer" as pseudo common sense because although the behaviors are expected, the signs offer direct language and thus leave no gray area for argument. However, what I see as common sense isn't always common sense. As we learned in the earlier chapters, cultural differences in perceptions of misbehavior and disrespect, along with family dynamics and learned behavior, can lead to misunderstandings. By using direct language in our signage, our rules and expectations will be clear to learners and other users of the school library space. If these signs are permanently posted, be sure to evaluate them either month to month or year to year. Outdated signs can invalidate or overshadow the ones that should be reinforced.

Depending on learners' demographics and areas of need, signage may need to be reevaluated with an added lens or two. While analyzing the space, it is vital to take the learners into consideration. If there is a high population of non-English speakers, signage needs to follow suit. Technology is available to translate flyers, signage, library rules, posters, displays, take-home materials, and any other resources provided to learners. Lean on educators in language departments to collaborate on translations or on reaching learners or families through more effective avenues. If there is a high population of learners with special needs, lean on fellow educators with experience in instructing learners with special needs or immerse yourself in the special needs community or professional development experiences focused on special needs. Seeking help and resources to better serve the school's population will only enhance your practice and your relationship with school library users (figure 0.3, II.B.A2).

Moving through the Space

The same advice offered in the preceding section should be noted when evaluating physical space. Our school library spaces aren't always mobile, flexible, or renovated, but think of the first steps toward accessibility. Think of the basics, no matter what era your space currently represents. Analyze the areas that are most heavily used. As you walk around the space, think about the ease with which you can get around. Notice areas that are hard to navigate, have inadequate lighting, or are hard to reach. If the space is currently exclusively able-bodied accessible, changes must be made to provide a space that is not only compliant with the Americans with Disabilities Act (ADA) but also welcoming for users with special needs and who are differently abled. If possible, it is beneficial for the school library space to have multiple inclusive seating options during instruction, programs, or free time. Consider options like floor seating, high seating, spaces for wheelchairs, spaces to stand, and rolling seats.

Our bookshelves and seating areas should offer different solutions for learners and fellow educators of all abilities. If the books on the bookshelves are occupying the very top shelf and learners are unable to reach their desired selections, then shifting or weeding the collection can alleviate their struggle. Doing this regularly not only further familiarizes us with our collection but also makes our collection accessible to short or wheelchair-bound learners. Another technique for making our bookshelves more interactive and the resources more accessible is the use of QR codes as signage. With the QR code linked to the e-book collection, databases, or other digital resources, learners can take a picture of the sign on the shelves and access materials digitally.

Much like the inclusion of QR code technology within the collection, other technologies can bring new services to the space. Adaptive technologies, in particular, may be a necessary investment for a more inclusive space depending on the school's population. Adaptive technologies range from small objects like magnifiers or adaptive mice to more advanced software like screen readers and text-to-speech synthesizers. If your budget doesn't allow for those enhancements, be sure to become familiar with community spaces that offer those technologies. Sending newsletters or monthly/quarterly e-mails to learners, other educators, and families offers us the opportunity to share not only school library resources but also information about community services and public access points. Fortunately, certain types of e-books and online databases already offer features that allow for a more comfortable reading experience with adjustable fonts and voice-over. Learners who need adaptive reading technology like increased font size, different font type, or voice-over capabilities can easily access e-books or online databases and take advantage of the features. Learning new technology offers us an opportunity to not only grow professionally but also connect with new and existing learners, whether in person or via video recording, by walking them through new inclusive features.

Permission to Take Up Space

Although our displays, signage, seating areas, and emerging/adaptive technologies elevate our spaces into inclusive, culturally responsive school libraries, the culture within the space is vital to making all those aspects fit in place and prove truly impactful. Building a culture that encourages exploration and self-empowerment can be done by fostering and nurturing trust and safety. Fostering and nurturing trust and safety is possible through constantly integrating culturally responsive practices and embracing inclusive room management skills. A helpful strategy that inherently relates to the root of our work as school librarians is the creation of "safe spaces" and "brave spaces" (figure 0.3, V.A.A2).

Safe Space

You may have heard the term *safe space* used in classrooms within your school, in professional development sessions, or in signage around your community. This term describes a space that is supportive and affirming of learners' identities. GLSEN (formerly the Gay, Lesbian and Straight Education Network), an organization whose mission is "to ensure that every member of every school community is valued and respected regardless of sexual orientation, gender identity or gender expression" (GLSEN 2022), offers other educators and learners a multitude of resources that can help create a safe, supportive, and LGBTQ+-inclusive environment. GLSEN defines a safe space as "a supportive and affirming environment for lesbian, gay, bisexual, trans/transgender, and queer (LGBTQ) students" (GLSEN, n.d.). Although it is virtually impossible to guarantee safety and affirmation for all learners throughout the entirety of the day, we must be consistent and intentional with our policies and expectations to ensure that our school library spaces are able to offer a respite from any outside environmental and personal stressors.

We have explored the concept of identity as it relates to our own experiences. With that knowledge, we can better understand the importance of affirming learner identities. That understanding, however, is not complete. It is vital to educate ourselves about identities that are different from ours. By educating ourselves through reading articles written and shared by organizations like GLSEN and Learning for Justice, we are better prepared to serve and welcome all learners and educators authentically into the school library space. It is our duty to continue our learning and professional development, especially when it comes to affirming identities and representing learners in all our work (figure 0.3, I.D.A2).

Part of that education includes creating actionable steps. As school librarians, we can create a safe space by learning about different identities and societal structures and creating norms and policies that advocate for inclusive, equitable, and non-discriminatory practices. When creating an environment that supports and affirms LGBTQ+ and marginalized identities, it is essential to understand gender identity, move away from our inclination to make assumptions, stay conscious of our bias, and be prepared to combat discrimination. After learning about and embracing the safe space elements via our own research and reading, we can post safe space stickers and posters on the doors or offices within the school library. Not only do these stickers and signs tell the school community that the school library is a welcoming and inclusive space, but they also share that you are available as a resource, an ally, and a confidant who advocates for privacy and will affirm all learners' identities, experiences, and pronouns.

Brave Space

Once the safe space is established and there is a sense of support and inclusion within the school library, there are ways to elevate learners' voices in a more active and intentional way. If you want to invite learners to participate in civil and productive conversations through a critical and responsive lens, a valuable practice to explore is the "brave space." In their article, "Safe Spaces, Brave Spaces and Why We Gon' Be Alright" (2019), Felicia Holman and Ellie Mejía wrote, "Brave spaces can look, sound and feel different from one another, but the general idea is to cultivate a productive dialogue where participants are encouraged to speak honestly and critically from their own experience toward the end of mutual learning and liberation." Because this is an emerging practice, if you are interested in nurturing this type of dialogue, it is essential to continue learning and seeking resources as the topic progresses.

As with safe spaces, the concept of brave spaces invites us to participate in elements that are already present in our profession. Brave spaces allow us to nurture learner voice in a way that challenges both ourselves and the learners. There are different approaches to creating and maintaining a brave space. The brave space can be formatted as a small discussion group, a school library advisory group, or a small-scale, open forum/town hall–type program within the school library (figure 0.3, II.C.A1). Having learners explore school library policy, the collection, and digital resources and then provide a constructive critical view or discuss how those elements apply to the greater community's needs can be an effective way to integrate the brave space practice. Utilizing smaller groups at the start of the process allows for closer relationships to develop within the group, which leads to the trust and openness that are essential for challenging conversations, especially if those conversations relate to race, identity, injustice, and sociopolitical views (figure 0.3, III.B.A2).

Being comfortable with discomfort is key to this experience, but that doesn't mean that there aren't guidelines to deter harmful discomfort or offense. Start by exploring inward, just like at the start of our culturally responsive journey. Then follow the lead of other practitioners like those referenced in the article by Holman and Mejía. They share sample agreements that can be helpful when setting up norms and expectations for the challenging conversations that may come up when inviting honest dialogue. Norms like "listen to understand, not to respond," "unpack the tension," "never be afraid to sit awhile and think," and "address the idea, not the person" allow for controversy with civility. The best aspect about safe space and brave space practices is that they offer opportunities for collaboration between learners and school librarians. Both practices involve vulnerability and honesty. They will strengthen our relationships with learners and other educators through open communication, an emphasis on constructive feedback, and a nurturing environment for civil activism (figure 0.3, VI.B.A1).

Making Time for Your Space

Whether you try one or all of these strategies, there will be a visible change to the space that comes with your courageous exploration. Incorporating new practices and learning from others who are doing the same does not have to happen overnight. These practices take time to establish, so don't feel pressured to have your physical space assessed, a safe space ready in the first month of returning to school, or a brave space established in the first year of trying. Taking moments to evaluate the space and creating a more welcoming and inclusive environment through smaller actionable steps are the right ways to go about making change. Smaller action steps like creating norms and displaying inclusive and culturally responsive books are perfect foundation steps for creating the safe space. As with anything in our profession, the initiatives we try need to make sense for our own school library space and our populations. Understanding that smaller intentional actions lay the foundation for larger, lasting impact is key to moving forward on this journey.

5

Thriving Partnerships

I t is common for school librarians to refer to themselves and one another as "islands" when talking about their positions in the school ecosystem. The reality is that, regardless of who occupies the space with us, being the only librarian in the school is lonely. School librarians fall into a hazy category of educator that includes instructor, materials support, counselor, activities coordinator, tech support, and secretary, not to mention our designated duties like budgeting, acquisitions, management, literacy, and more. Because we wear many demanding hats, the time that would otherwise be used for outreach can easily be filled with another, more pressing task. I would argue that even if we had a lifeboat to take us to the mainland, there is too much happening on the island to consider leaving. Although there is no easy solution, there are some areas of outreach that vary in time commitment and would work well within our culturally responsive framework.

Prized Partnerships in Your District

Partnerships within your school building or district are great ways to explore outreach on your own terms and availability. Whether you have ten minutes or an entire class period to dedicate to a specific educator or group, forging relationships like these will help you put culturally responsive strategies and perspectives into practice. Three types of partnerships within your school district that may be worth exploring or that you may already be nurturing are partnerships with other educators, with other school librarians (if there are any others), and with affinity groups within your building.

School Librarian + Other Educators

The partnership between yourself and other educators is incredibly beneficial, as you know, not only for creating valuable collaboration opportunities but also for increasing awareness of the school library's services and resources. This partnership may seem like a common-sense suggestion, but there are more areas to explore within it. Thinking back on the reflective activities and introspective practices discussed at the beginning of this book, we can start to identify areas of study that can shift to include culturally responsive-sustaining ideals. Start with the content area that you are most comfortable supporting. Then think of ways in which the subject matter can include culturally responsive topics. In which ways can lessons, units, resources, and assignments include a more diverse set of populations? For example, in an English/reading class, most of the book selections for a traditional curriculum are "classics." These are books that are renowned and often used year after year. Classic American literature lends itself to the study of literary analysis, plot devices, character tropes, and so forth because it is so heavily analyzed. Resources for these books are readily available and easily accessible to learners and educators.

As we explore culturally responsive practices and identify our ever-moving place on the continuum of cultural proficiency, we must push ourselves to embrace discomfort and urge others to explore as well. By expanding our reading choices, understanding perspectives other than our own, and seeing the value of contemporary young adult fiction, we can share our findings with English/reading educators and supplement their lessons with rich texts that fit their curriculum criteria. Highlighting authors and characters who identify as neurodiverse, LGBTQ+, persons of color, and any other identification that is traditionally marginalized is essential, beyond being "culturally responsive" (figure 0.3, IV.A.A2). Representing learners' experiences and exposing them to differing experiences are vital to raising learner interest, voice, and empathy. When instructors are open but hesitant to supplement their lessons with new titles, it is usually due to curriculum pressures, time limitations, or general unawareness of new titles. Encouraging educators to embrace the unknown can be facilitated by reassuring them that these texts will not replace the classics, unless that's the goal, but instead will add to the examination of literary devices and analysis studied in the classics by providing a modern look into modern situations.

Consider the following approaches to lay the groundwork for thriving partnerships with other educators in your learning community:

- Collaborate with another educator with whom you feel most comfortable. This person can become your partner in growth, and the result may empower you to try again with others.
- Offer suggestions for ways to incorporate contemporary texts or modern classics as supplemental resources to curriculum materials.

- Prepare booklists that learners and other educators can access passively to gain awareness about the culturally diverse collection.
- Prepare focused booklists that detail possible titles and descriptions as they relate to a particular unit. For example, if the class is discussing poetic verse, scan the shelves or local public library offerings for contemporary books of verse. Titles like these come to mind: *Long Way Down* by Jason Reynolds, *The Poet X* by Elizabeth Acevedo, *Swing* by Kwame Alexander, and *The Truth Project* by Dante Medema.
- If time permits, collaborate on an independent reading unit that includes a book tasting in the school library. Such an event showcases books that may expand learner perspectives and help them engage authentically and with interest in topics like plot analysis.

School Librarian + Other School Librarians

Life on the school librarian island becomes less lonely when we realize that our island is actually part of a populated archipelago. The truth of the matter is that though the archipelago may span the country, not every school district is equipped with the same kinds of islands. Some school districts have only one school librarian, others have a school librarian in each school, and still others, unfortunately, have no school librarian at all. If your school district is one in which you are the sole librarian, prioritizing outreach may seem like a waste of time because you are already inundated with task after task, but it may prove just the opposite. Understanding the resources, avenues, and outlets around you can make your life easier. Knowing that you have a professional ally close by is refreshing when you are feeling like no one can relate.

If the opportunity exists within your school district to work with school librarians of different grade levels, make the time to take advantage of it. They are working with learners from the same community, can share their data with you, and can help brainstorm strategies for tackling tough issues and tough-to-connect-with educators. For example, I was finding it difficult to bridge a connection with the other school librarians in the district. The school librarian in the middle school had similar feelings, so she created a one-page district-wide library newsletter in hopes of enticing everyone with a low-stakes, collaborative outreach project. We all met virtually to discuss one quick highlight from that month/season that coincides with an AASL Standards Domain (Think, Create, Share, and Grow) or an ALA theme. That meeting was a great excuse and opportunity to chat with colleagues who understand our specific dilemmas and can celebrate the wins. This interactive, friendly, and quick get-together also gave us a chance to highlight the great work we were each doing that often goes unnoticed. Forming partnerships like these removed intimidation and the excuse of time limitations and opened doors for more innovative and engaging projects between schools (figure 0.3, V.C.A1).

There are also hundreds of school librarians on islands all over the country. Exploring our professional networks and making connections is vital to progressing our careers. Seeing what innovative ideas people are trying and the ways that colleagues are addressing and overcoming situations that puzzle you will improve your practice. Joining professional organizations or becoming a member of professional groups on social platforms can open the floodgates for ideas and perspectives. There is also a sense of activist agency when witnessing situations like book banning, legislative actions, and staff dismissals. Being aware of situations that harm not only our profession but also the lives of our learners can empower us to put in the time and effort for this work and fight back against censorship.

School Librarian + Affinity Groups

Affinity groups are groups formed around shared interests or goals. These groups can be formally and informally present in our school communities. Affinity groups are also commonly referred to as clubs. Learners with shared interests can be extremely passionate, which is helpful when curating materials and experiences for them. Given their zeroed-in interests, it is easier to suggest books, plan programs, and collaborate on advocacy efforts. Creating a partnership with affinity groups can also expand comfort and trust between yourself, the learners, and the school library (figure 0.3, VI.C.A1). That comfort and trust will, it is hoped, translate into increased circulation, feedback, and morale within the space. Having a group of learners who feel comfortable visiting the school library and exploring titles on their own time can lead to their cooperation when gathering feedback on matters like school library policies and room climate.

If your school has a Genders & Sexualities Alliance or Queer–Straight Alliance, for example, you can create a booktalk and share resources and materials for and about the LGBTQ+ community with the group. Sharing community resources can be a great way to connect learners with outside organizations that can further nurture their inquiry. As we know, reading is a great way to explore sensitive topics in the safety and privacy of one's mind. Learners will be able to explore relationships, friendships, and circumstances that are portrayed by characters that they can relate to and aren't always readily accessible. Sharing resources or planning programs can help put a face to your name and show the learners that you are there to support and assist in their inquiry. Other examples of affinity groups that you might see in your school building are an Asian American/Pacific Islander Appreciation Club, a Black Student Union, a Fashion Club, a Dungeons and Dragons Club, an Activist Club, and so on. If you aren't sure about joining or collaborating with any specific group, it may be easier to contact the advisor and ask if they would be interested in using one of their club meetings to explore the school library. Inviting learners, some of whom wouldn't normally visit the school library, into the space can expand their perspective about the library's offerings and, we hope, make them feel safe visiting the space in the future.

CHALLENGE: AFFINITY GROUP INVOLVEMENT

» Can you identify any affinity groups in your building that you can visit with to gain new perspectives?
» Can you identify any affinity groups in your building that would benefit from being introduced to culturally diverse titles?
» Can you identify any affinity groups in your building that can offer suggestions for titles that focus on differing perspectives and populations?

Prized Partnerships in Your Community

Community and culture go hand in hand. Understanding the cultural and racial makeup of learners and their guardians as well as that of the town itself can lead to more responsive partnerships and services. Exploring partnerships between the community and the school library can start in familiar territory and expand to unknown areas. If exploring resources outside the school setting is new to you, start with the public library. Public libraries house librarians who understand your profession, drive, and interests as they relate to the services provided to learners (figure 0.3, III.A.A2). If you already partner with local libraries, explore how that partnership can grow through programs like job search assistance for high schoolers or read-aloud sessions for elementary schoolers or after-school programs for middle schoolers. If you are ready to explore the community with a wider lens, try community groups. Community groups offer valuable resources for learners and their families as well as possible cultural connections that can lead to trust and comfort.

School Librarian + Public Libraries

Ensuring equitable access to materials is a difficult task. Accessibility to resources can be impeded by anything from school closures to school library closures for testing/ class visits/equipment repairs to technology deficiencies to school board censorship attempts to budgetary restraints, and more. We do our best to provide the services and materials needed for each learner, but it is impossible to control what we can't or don't have the authority to regulate. For those reasons, setting up fail-safes through outside partnerships will guarantee continued access for learners whether they are in the building or not. Fostering a partnership with local public libraries not only supplements your collection when budgets are tight and ordering only happens a couple of times a year but also expands the services you can direct learners to (figure 0.3, III.D.A2).

Some examples of public library services are job search support, citizenship classes, English language classes, interactive and enjoyable programming aimed at young adults, free wireless internet access, designated quiet spaces, and social work counselors. Most public librarians and staff members also have an open-minded approach to serving the public. People of all walks of life step into the public library every day to receive valued services, which should make it easier for the learners in your school to find an ally there. Public libraries offer users increased access to books, technology, and public services as well as a welcoming space when our schools are closed. Given public libraries' larger budgets for acquisitions and less outside control over book selections, learners can explore their interests beyond what's on our school library shelves. The possibilities are endless when learners are able to feel comfortable within their schools and out in the community.

Consider the following approaches to lay the groundwork for thriving partnerships with public libraries in your local community:

- Subscribe to the public library's newsletter and share relevant items with learners.
- Invite the Youth Services/Young Adult/Teen librarian to present a booktalk, either in person or virtually. This event can take place during a lunch period, study hall, or after school or be posted on an online platform for convenient access.
- Host a local public library employee for a library card sign-up day/week. Public library employees can provide learners information about their services and bring books and promotional materials with them to the school building. If hosting at the school building is not possible, perhaps the public library employee can set up a table at a school-sponsored sports/academic event or join learners at a community event.
- If time permits, join county, regional, state-wide, or national librarian associations (many of which have youth services sections) to meet, in person or virtually, and collaborate with librarians of all disciplines.

School Librarian + Community Groups

Partnering with community groups within your town or county takes time and commitment. It may not be your first priority when starting the year in comparison to planning instructional lessons, but these partnerships can be valuable in our culturally responsive journey. Similar to the public library partnership, fostering or strengthening a relationship with community groups increases learner access to services and resources that would otherwise go unnoticed (figure 0.3, III.A.P2). Community groups are able to offer services that focus on cultural and socioeconomic necessities in ways that are not possible in the school setting. Unless you are passionate about the community group, you don't have to act as an advocate or recruiter. Instead the school library can act as an information hub for relevant resources and helpful materials.

The process of creating partnerships with community groups can start by doing research or asking others for advice on worthwhile organizations. The guidance department or special services department most likely already has many resources like handouts, brochures, important phone numbers, and websites. Asking for those resources and displaying them intentionally for learners to grab with passive or deliberate interest shows that the school library is a partner in learner well-being and success.

Consider the following approaches to foster or strengthen a partnership with community organizations:

- Subscribe to the organization's newsletter and share relevant items with learners.
- If the community group is interested, create a booklist for their members that can be featured on their website or online platforms. This collaboration can position you as an advocate for literacy and culturally responsive texts within the community. For example, if there is an Italian Heritage Association in the community, highlight books written by Italian authors and about the Italian experience. The same suggestion can apply to many other groups.
- Collaborate with the community group's outreach staff members to house a resource list on the school library's online platform.
- If possible, invite a guest speaker, in person or virtually, from the community group to read poetry or a passage from a book that fits with their group's identity. Schedule or record these events during designated times of the year or as a series. Allowing community group speakers to participate in literacy initiatives also offers learners a familiar person at the organization to reach out to as needed. This suggestion may provide a valuable connection between parents/families, school library resources, and community groups in the area (figure 0.3, V.C.P2).

Outreach in Ways That Make Sense

Partnerships are not a one-size-fits-all situation. Inviting the community into your space takes proper consideration and time. Those two things are not always at our disposal. As mentioned, these partnerships do not have to happen overnight, nor do they have to all happen at once. Start where you feel comfortable, and make a plan to foster or strengthen relationships as they make sense for you, your community, your learners, and the school library. Sharing resources and signing up for newsletters are the best first steps in understanding different groups within your learning community and local community and their offerings (figure 0.3, II.C.A2). Another possible first step is to chat with departments in your school building that regularly connect learners with outside resources. Regardless of whether you are experiencing certain partnerships for the first time or you are a seasoned partner, expanding your work to highlight inclusive and culturally relevant materials will benefit learners and the partners you are working with.

PART III

Learner

6

Active Participants

As school librarians, we have the unique skill set of working within five different professional roles all at once. Our information specialist and program administrator roles focus on our school community's interests, access to information and resources, connecting with a global learning community, maintaining our school library's budget, and so on. Our instructional partner and educator roles focus on collaboration and instructing learners according to interests, standards, curriculum, and structures. Last but not least, our role as leader is sometimes the most subtle but also the most impactful role we take on. By modeling culturally responsive practices, we exemplify our "increased professional commitment and thorough knowledge of the challenges and opportunities facing the profession" (AASL 2018, 14).

We navigate between our roles every day, prioritizing different roles daily depending on schedules, demands, and learner needs. When we take on the role of instructor, all the roles converge. Through our inward explorations, we now carry culturally responsive practices with us in the way that we reflect, collaborate, and organize our school libraries and, of course, in our instruction. Whether instruction comes in the form of regular classes, specials on a rotating schedule, inviting classes into the space for specific lessons, or collaborating with educators on exciting initiatives, there are numerous opportunities to integrate culturally responsive aspects into our lessons. Supplementing your lessons with these strategies should be done with intention and as appropriate for your lesson style, with enough room for modification and flexibility.

Class Culture

Do not worry if you already have structures in place or if you are reading this during the middle of the school year. The practices we will be discussing are not exclusively applicable for the beginning of the school year. If you are trying these methods in the middle of your school year, try mixing some of the practices or strategies presented here into your already planned lessons or units. Starting a new unit with one new strategy may make implementation less overwhelming. As said throughout this journey, there are no boxes to check off and no true end point, only constant learning, growing, and improving as people and as school librarians. This is important to keep in mind because as we know with instruction, what worked one year may not work the next, and there is always room for modification and flexibility.

The culturally responsive journey starts within us and then is transferred to our lessons, school library spaces, collections, and practices. Introducing certain practices into instruction, like this whole journey, starts at the beginning and at your own pace. Just as we had to explore inward and approach new terms and principles with an open mind, so will the learners. Using the principles we learned and integrating new strategies, we can provide learners with a helpful structure they can follow throughout the school year. Learners are already used to introducing themselves and sharing their interests with their peers at the start of every new school year. They are primed for illustrating this type of introductory picture of their identity, which provides us the foundation needed to support exploration and illustration at new levels and with greater frequency.

Before encouraging learners to explore inward and share outward, reiterate the importance of the norms you created and hold in highest regard. Whether norms were previously labeled class rules or expectations, it is key that learners understand that norms exist to ensure the physical and emotional safety of everyone in the instructional setting, including the school librarian. If your class rules are already solidly in place, consider adding a few norms that make sense (figure 0.3, I.A.A2). Adding direct language like "respect others—their similarities and differences" and "listen to understand, not to respond" deters miscommunication and builds a trusting environment for authentic dialogue. The norms you originally created will change as the year progresses, as new learners enter the class, and as learners take a more active role in the discussion structure.

CHALLENGE: NORM BREACH

Violations or breaches of shared norms are likely to occur. We can approach shared norms like we would our classroom rules. Reflective exercises and assignments that are more personal in nature require vulnerability from our learners. We can safeguard learners from ridicule or judgment through our actions. Our responses to norm breaches and poor behaviors should be quick, thoughtful, and effective (figure O.3, III.C.P2, III.C.A2).

» How would we react or respond to a learner who steps out of line and says something unexpected and unacceptable?

» Do we have a go-to line we use to rein in disturbances that can be adapted to addressing norm breaches?

» How can we adapt our "script" to respond to harmful language or behaviors?

Consider these approaches for safeguarding learners and responding to negative situations:

» Implement a protocol whereby learners can signal when a phrase is hurtful during discussions using a code word like "ouch," "yikes," or "yeesh." These words are best used during open discussion sessions, not during lectures or learner-led presentations so as to not create an environment where interruptions are expected or encouraged.

» Introduce a folder in which learners can find and submit a physical or electronic form privately when they feel hurt or confused by another learner or subject matter during discussions. This strategy will also provide learners a way to ask for your help or pinpoint uncomfortable situations while avoiding judgment or drawing attention to themselves. These situations can be addressed as you feel appropriate.

» Use direct phrases or explanations to respond quickly, thoughtfully, and effectively to avoid derailing the lesson or making situations more personal than necessary. If something offensive is said or one of the norms is breached, addressing the situation by naming the behavior and saying why it is unacceptable will deter any misunderstandings and, we hope, future incidents.

After you have ensured that the norms are understood and have pinpointed behaviors that are unacceptable in the space, learners can begin to share openly and feel like they have permission to be their authentic selves in your class and in their classwork.

Exploring inward and sharing outward are valuable processes that will benefit learners both inside and outside the classroom. As learners begin to explore their identities and values, those aspects will transfer over to their work. Trust will form within the space, dialogues will be more authentic, and increased interest will lead to an engaged group of learners. Familiarizing learners with reflective strategies throughout the school year is vital as we explore and implement culturally responsive practices in the common areas of school library instruction like digital literacy, research methods, and independent reading/selection (figure 0.3, I.A.A1). Learning more about our learners through reflective strategies and their work will make it easier to identify shared and differing cultural reference viewpoints on respect, authority, praise/shame, and collaboration (figure 0.3, III.A.P1). Expanding our perspectives of each learner based on their interests, identities, and values will provide us the tools for forging stronger bonds, engaging in more effective communication, and creating culturally responsive assignments.

Learners Looking Inward

Having learners fill out identity gardens at the start of the school year or a new unit will provide them a structure to explore their identity and begin to better understand reflective practices. Learners can fill in the circles with their identity markers as they feel comfortable, without pressure to complete each circle. The identity gardens categories can be modified as appropriate for grade level or maturity of class. They should offer a closer look into a learner's identity, without causing distress. Dedicate a few minutes to encouraging learners to share one or two of their identity markers with the class—learners can take ownership of what they see as the "most important" aspects of their identity, and the class can gain new perspectives about their peers. The aspects that learners choose to share may be something they readily present or something that would have gone unnoticed otherwise. This type of introspection and sharing activity can take the place of a check-in or "do now" activity during a couple of days within a designated week. The identity gardens can be collected after each check-in time and passed back out at the start of the class period until everyone who feels comfortable sharing is able to share. Before the final check-in day, make copies of the learners' identity gardens and keep them in a secure place. After returning the identity gardens to the learners, you will have a copy to reference as needed throughout the school year. You can revisit the identity gardens throughout the school year to add notes about individual learners, as you normally would, but this time, you will have an idea of how each learner self-identifies and how they present themselves. The identity gardens can set a foundation for your notes, offer you valuable cultural and social information, and remove any opportunity for preconceived assumptions.

Nurturing this sense of exploration and reflection can be helpful before starting new units and throughout lessons. Before starting new units, when we are introducing learners to unfamiliar terms and concepts, we can use techniques to gauge personal comfort levels, prejudices, and perceptions about the subject matter. This practice does not necessarily change our planned unit structure or lesson plans, which are sometimes inflexible because of testing and standards. Instead, the practice will help learners get used to viewing new concepts and subject matter with a critical and reflective lens. We can provide learners dedicated time, during "do now" time, when they can privately reflect on a K-W-L Chart graphic organizer. A K-W-L Chart allows learners the opportunity to track what they *know* (K) about the topic, what they *want* (W) to know, and finally what they *learned* (L). Adapting the widely used K-W-L Chart graphic organizer to include *why* (W) learners know about the topic and *how* (H) they will find the information will add some context to their initial thoughts on the topic (figure 0.3, I.B.P1). Diving into why learners may have been aware of the topic, whether from personal experience or through outside influence, may be a terrific way to better understand their exposure to certain topics (figure 6.1, shown on the following page). Learners can revisit their thoughts and reflect on their initial perception of the topic once they have completed the lesson or unit and then learned from it (figure 0.3, I.B.A1).

The KWWHL Chart and other reflective exercises are useful because they allow us to better understand why learners are either excited or apprehensive about certain lessons or our projected units for the year. Sometimes the apprehension comes from preconceived notions that can stem from societal or cultural viewpoints. Sometimes it is based on disinterest. Sometimes it is caused by general lack of self-confidence about the topic. In any case, gaining insight into the reasons can help us navigate learners toward success more responsively. Whether you have learners analyze every new lesson, theme, or unit in this way or try incorporating an analytical approach only with big subject shifts, adding reflective exercises like these will provide you and the learner valuable insight.

Reflecting on Research Strategies

Our approach to our research strategies and digital literacy lessons can also benefit from a critical reflective lens. Adding reflective practices into everyday lessons allows for more culturally responsive searches, selections, assignments, and assessments.

FIGURE 6.1

KWWHL Chart example

TOPIC: Media Bias

What do you *know*?	Media bias sounds like it has to do with the way news is written.
Why **do you know about the topic?**	I have heard people on TV and online say "fake news." This could mean that the news is wrong. Maybe this is part of media bias?
What do you *want* **to know?**	Why is media bias such a big deal? Does it really matter where news comes from if it is all saying the same thing?
How **will you find information?**	I will use the databases that the school librarian is telling us about.
What have you *learned*?	I learned that media bias is more than what information is shared. It is about where the information is coming from, what influences those sources, the type of emotion or action they want from the reader or viewer, and how that information gets shared.

When we invite ourselves and our learners to analyze search strategies and research topic selections, we encourage the exploration of reflexive habits and bias in a way that connects to the world outside the instructional environment (figure 0.3, IV.A.P1). Themes of bias and misperception are common threads in digital literacy lessons. Those themes allow for a natural integration of culturally responsive practices. We should highlight opportunities for learners to think about the critical choices they make when consuming and using information (figure 0.3, I.B.P1). Taking advantage of reflective practices in the form of prompts or casual discussion will allow learners to think critically about what sources they visit and why, as well as why they consume the types of information they do.

Learners should take ownership of their information consumption much the same as they do their entertainment (figure 0.3, IV.A.A1). Now, more than ever, they are living an extremely information-rich life. The information and entertainment that they have at their fingertips pose situations that are positive, negative, and everything in between. Learners are experiencing life through photos and videos and sharing those experiences with others at a speed quicker than ever before. Trends last a millisecond, learners' lives are on display in ways that make it hard to separate virtual and real, and misinformation runs rampant on both ends of the spectrum. It is valuable for learners to understand what lives behind the images, articles, and videos they consume. We can boost that understanding by dedicating time for learners to pinpoint the sites that they visit regularly, research the parent company of the publication, and understand how those companies or creators influence the amount of exposure that images, articles, and videos receive on timelines through advertising budgets and company status.

Although our focus doesn't entail managing learners' exposure or use, we can offer them tools to safeguard themselves from potential misinformation or bias-driven information consumption habits in the future (figure 0.3, II.B.A1). Tools and strategies found in our regularly planned digital literacy lessons can be supplemented with resources that discuss media bias, echo chambers, virtue signaling, confirmation bias, motivated reasoning, sensationalism, misinformation, disinformation, and marginalized voices. Although these concepts are all part of the digital literacy landscape, learners may not be aware of the many layers involved in media creation and dissemination, which ultimately influences what they regularly see online.

As we try to boost learner awareness through reflection, we must also turn the practice inward. As always in this journey, it is key to look inward when new concepts are involved. Our natural habits and reflexive actions go unchecked if we do not take time to step back and reflect. Sometimes small changes to our demo lessons, examples, or prompts can make our lessons more culturally responsive and inclusive. For example, when I began reflecting on the examples used to demonstrate database features and functions, it was clear that the authors used in my examples did not match learner interest and could be supplemented with more culturally responsive choices (figure 0.3, V.A.P1). Although I still showed learners how to find biographical information about William Shakespeare, I also demonstrated other features like character analysis and essay prompts related to contemporary authors, especially authors of color, like Elizabeth Acevedo and Zadie Smith. Similar shifts can be attempted with other content areas by demonstrating research strategies with the focus on prolific scientists or historical events of varied cultural backgrounds and identities.

These shifts in our chosen examples do not change the format or function of our demonstrations. Instead, we are using our platform and position of power to subtly showcase marginalized voices. We hope that learners will see this as inspiration and permission to explore influential figures of varied cultural backgrounds and identities to supplement their understanding of the lesson. Likewise, when we share these resources with other educators, we should aim to involve texts and resources that challenge convention, mirror student experience, and allow for deeper discussion on the subject matter.

Highlighting Choice

As learners become more familiar with reflective practices, they will feel more comfortable making decisions that impact their educational experience. They will know more about themselves and their choices. Nurturing learner voice is a priority not only in the school library profession but also when on the culturally responsive journey. Integrating learner voice into the classroom management structure and into reflective practices leads to shared trust and accountability. By valuing learners' developing voices and challenging them to make choices within the assignments and assessments, we can help learners have increased ownership and interest in their work.

There are two aspects of choice that learners can take advantage of. Choice as it relates to assignment topic is slightly more complicated than choice in the assignment format (figure 0.3, I.C.A2). Learner choice in the assignment topic should be contained within parameters that make sense for the assignment. Encourage learners to choose through a more inclusive lens by providing examples in the assignment prompt that may interest them, like texts, figures, or events that involve individuals who have various cultural identities and abilities. Learners should also find support through their inclusive research exploration in the materials on the school library shelves, book displays, and digital resources. Some examples of assignment format choices are filming or animating short videos, recording verbal responses or mock podcasts, casting a movie based on characters, selecting songs for a playlist based on characters or historical/story events, creating mock social media accounts for figures, creating a visual presentation, or completing standard assignment formats like essays or tests on paper if technology is not accessible.

Growing as a Group

At the crux of the strategies we have discussed is the importance of shared learning experiences in a safe environment. The school library is the perfect space for such experiences. Regardless of how our school libraries are structured, they house vital entertainment and information resources, offer immense knowledge about information gathering, and are primed for group work whether casually or formally. As shared meeting spaces, school libraries offer an open and safe environment for social and educational lessons to be learned. When we explore societal norms and offer resources addressing public services and displaying different social situations, we equip learners with passive information that can be used or modified for their own needs. As instructors, when we group learners together and encourage open dialogue and rich discussions, our aim is to have learners learn from each other.

Strategies to encourage shared learning through instruction should include methods like intentional and accountable collaborative group work and shared forums for new ideas and discussions. Using collaborative group work exercises as a way for learners to teach their peers not only holds each member accountable but also offers up different perspectives on the one topic of choice (figure 0.3, III.B.P1). Having learners teach their peers offers a sense of ownership of the topic they researched, and more-authentic discussions can take place as questions arise. Shared forums can be displayed in person and digitally (figure 0.3, V.B.A2). One example of a shared forum is a "new to me" board (figure 0.3, III.A.A1). Create a publicly shared, yet anonymous, "new to me" board to display new perspectives gained specifically from peers' presentations and collaborative work. This board can be adopted physically, like an area on a whiteboard, or virtually on a shared forum or document. This board will be especially useful as assignments take on different forms. Another example is a prompt on a digital classroom space. Building a space in which learners can share their input within a more casual discussion-based format provides an opportunity for extension and application of lesson topics through the lens of their personal experiences and perspectives.

Learning from others is possible when our minds are open and when we value the perspectives of others. Those qualities are nurtured in a safe environment through the culturally responsive and inclusive practices that we are trying, adapting, and integrating in our spaces throughout this journey.

7

Scenarios

Our journey will lead us into situations that we may not have encountered before, some requiring more consideration and finesse than others. Acting through scenarios allows us to observe the application of the concepts and skills discussed. All the scenarios feature school librarians or assistants interacting with learners, educators, or their community. The scenarios also feature an area highlighting an imagined inner conflict and an area that pinpoints the harm that can stem from unaddressed situations. Each scenario is also presented with its connection to the Shared Foundation and Domain in relation to the *AASL Standards Frameworks Applied to Culturally Responsive Practice* (figure 0.3). Although these are not all-encompassing predictors of possible situations that can occur when embracing and applying culturally responsive principles, they do offer real-world context for our individual contemplation.

Curate, Share | Elementary School

The Situation: Keeping an Eye on the Collection

During his regularly scheduled read-aloud time, school librarian Mr. Daniel notices that two learners, not related, are having a hard time following the story. Every so often, the learners ask Mr. Daniel to repeat words and seem defeated after the words are repeated. They also have a hard time finding books during independent reading time. Mr. Daniel is in constant conversation with the educators of this grade level, so he knows that this is regular behavior for the two learners. He wants to dig deeper and help make the school library more responsive to their needs. When Mr. Daniel asks the learners about the books they have at home, Eddy and Joey share Korean and French titles. After taking some time to analyze the books on the school library shelves, Mr. Daniel notices that not only are the books only in English but the non-fiction collection is lacking books about different cultures.

Internal Conflict

Mr. Daniel understands that Eddy and Joey are struggling when it comes to connecting to the stories that he reads during class. He can think of some instructional modifications he can make during and after his read-alouds to support Eddy, Joey, and any other confused learners in understanding the books easier. He finds it overwhelming, however, when he begins to think about the work he needs to do with the collection. He is worried that he will not find sufficiently representative books.

What Is the Harm?

Culturally responsive practices urge school librarians to understand their learners as individuals and appreciate the experiences that learners bring into the school library. In this case, Mr. Daniel observed the behaviors of his learners and sought out more information from them to better understand where the disconnect began. If he had attributed Eddy's and Joey's actions and disinterest to misbehavior, there would be no change in the situation. The school library would continue to serve some of the learners instead of striving to reach more. If Mr. Daniel does nothing about this situation, not much will change. If he, instead, intentionally chooses to break down his overwhelming feelings with feasible small solutions, he can begin to better understand his learners, expand his professional network, and engage families as richly cultural partners.

Strategies for Repairing the Climate

Mr. Daniel is ready to incorporate more culturally responsive activities in his instruction methods. He started the school year by creating shared norms and has hung engaging, inclusive signage in the school library space. Now that he has firsthand experience with understanding new identities during class instruction, he can introduce the identity garden activity. Because the learners who visit the school library are young, he can adapt the template to limit the options. For example, he can provide learners four different identity marker options to choose from. He can choose markers like "name with pronunciation," "favorite color," "family unit," and "spoken languages."

This information will guide Mr. Daniel in his collection analysis and acquisition. He can access formal collection audits on school library software that can provide insight into gaps in the fiction and nonfiction selection. Mr. Daniel can find responsive titles on websites like *School Library Journal*, EmbraceRace, and Common Sense Media and through professional networks. He can also reach out to families of learners for suggestions of titles in other languages based on the ones they have at home. Building and nurturing a relationship with families that gives value to their cultural backgrounds will reinforce culturally responsive practices in the school library. Mr. Daniel should keep in mind that buying responsive titles and updating his collection will take time. There is no expected timeline or set list of cultural boxes to check off. Learners benefit from seeing themselves, their friends, their families, and their communities, and Mr. Daniel can create those opportunities one step at a time.

Engage, Share | Middle School

The Situation: Taking a Closer Look

School librarian Ms. Ambrose is on track to support an English educator's lesson by preparing a booktalk and booklist for an upcoming independent reading unit. She decided that the best way to understand learners in the class was to sit in on the collaborating educator's lesson. The first day she sat in, she noticed that all the examples that her partner presented were of books written in the 1980s and 1990s by white authors about white characters. Most learners in the class were visibly disinterested. Ms. Ambrose decides to send out an anonymous survey to learners in the class to get a better picture of their interests and honest opinions about their reading habits. Actively listening to learners through the survey showed that learners, like Ann and Francis, do not see themselves in the books that they read in class and do not believe that there are books accessible to them that represent their experiences.

Internal Conflict

Although Ms. Ambrose knows that those books exist in her school library, she is also aware that learner exposure to books and literacy begins in the classroom. If they are disinterested in examples during the lessons, they might be deterred from visiting the school library, which lessens their access to exceptional stories.

Ms. Ambrose wants to avoid overstepping on the collaborating educator's lesson. She knows that middle schoolers are at an important crossroad in their literacy journey. She also knows that learners may be reluctant to stray from the examples presented during the lessons, even if they do not like the choices. This type of familiarity and then disinterest creates an unproductive cycle for reluctant readers.

What Is the Harm?

Ms. Ambrose prides herself on intentionally including an assortment of inclusive and culturally responsive titles in her presentations and booklists, but she is aware of the disconnect regarding curriculum texts and popular examples. It is vital for learners to see themselves, their friends, and their communities in the books they have access to, regardless of what they enjoy reading. Providing access is key. Ms. Ambrose feels like learners are at a disadvantage if she only provides the class with booktalks and booklists without addressing her perspectives with the collaborating educator and the department. Because everyone is avoiding these conversations, the issues will continue year after year.

After the Cooperative Children's Book Center (CCBC) released its 2019 survey results about representation in books, Madeline Tyner (2020, n.p.) wrote,

> Despite slow progress, the number of books featuring BIPOC protagonists lags far behind the number of books with white main characters—or even those with animal or other characters. Taken together, books about white children, talking bears, trucks, monsters, potatoes, etc. represent nearly three quarters (71%) of children's and young adult books published in 2019.

Encouraging learners to seek out and gain access to books that are culturally responsive and representative of a variety of identities and experiences will positively impact their reading habits.

Strategies for Expanding Perspectives

Ms. Ambrose can be transparent from the very beginning to ease nerves and strengthen the collaboration. After sitting in on the lesson, she can schedule a meeting with her collaborating educator and let them know the game plan for their partnership. Ms. Ambrose can share the survey and the results and discuss the importance of learner insight regarding interests and reading habits. If the collaborating educator is aware of how the disparity in book selection creates disinterest in their learners, then Ms. Ambrose can suggest updating the lesson presentation examples or offer her creative skills to help with the updated slides. If not, Ms. Ambrose and the other educator are already on the same page regarding the lesson plan and activities, which should offer an easy entrance to the more serious conversation about underrepresentation and awareness. She can share strategies, resources, and data about inclusive book selections to help alleviate hesitation and stress.

Collaborate, Share | High School

The Situation: Quickly and Clearly

While walking toward the back of the school library with a cart full of books to reshelve, school librarian Ms. Campbell-Bertollo overhears a group of learners chatting about their weekend activities. She continues to shelve as they discuss but stops immediately when she hears some seriously troubling language. Having followed the examples of creating and displaying library norms, she knows that there is signage posted about appropriate behavior, zero tolerance for hate speech, and mutual respect. When she approaches the group, she sees that Mario is the person responsible. While chatting, he called many activities and other learners an offensive and hate-filled term.

Internal Conflict

Ms. Campbell-Bertollo likes to keep a friendly atmosphere in the school library. She does not feel confident reprimanding Mario and is scared that the conversation will cause a scene. She is also scared that the interaction will lead to those learners avoiding the school library.

What Is the Harm?

While Mario is speaking, Ms. Campbell-Bertollo sees two regulars, Jane and Charlie, look down at their palms and start fidgeting in their chairs. Jane looks over at Charlie and, to comfort him, lightly touches his shoulder. Charlie gets up from his seat, dejected, and leaves the library while Mario continues this story.

It is understandable that Ms. Campbell-Bertollo is worried about alienating learners who might stop using the space, but at the same time, she is letting her hesitance stop her from protecting Charlie and the other learners from harmful prejudice.

Strategies for Repairing the Climate

Here are two possible paths to take in this situation.

> Path 1: Ms. Campbell-Bertollo overhears Mario calling many activities and other learners the offensive and hate-filled term. She immediately approaches the table and interjects in a calm and respectful manner. She asks the learners to pay attention as she says, "I am sorry to interrupt, but that type of language is not appropriate nor welcome here. There

are helpful reminders around the room in case you forget. Please apologize to your friends. If you continue to use hateful language, you will have to leave the library and go to the principal's office."

Path 2: Ms. Campbell-Bertollo overhears Mario calling many activities and other learners the offensive and hate-filled term. She immediately approaches the table and interjects in a calm and respectful manner. She asks to speak to Mario, telling him to follow her to her desk. Once at her desk, away from the others, she tells Mario that his behavior and language will not be tolerated in the school library because they might hurt the feelings of other learners. He reassures her that it will not happen again, and he goes back to the table. Ms. Campbell-Bertollo feels like she saw something and said something, but she has a sneaky suspicion that this will not be the last time this disrespect will happen.

Both paths are feasible and valid, but one will encourage change. In both strategies Ms. Campbell-Bertollo immediately addresses Mario in a respectful manner and names the negative behavior. The differences between the approaches are accountability and consequence factors. Path 1 uses direct language, points Mario toward library policy, asks him to be accountable by apologizing, provides support for other learners, and presents Mario with future consequences. Path 2 removes Mario from his peers, does not point to policy, alludes to the consequence of harmful actions instead of holding Mario accountable for hurting feelings, and does not mention consequences of continued behavior. If the behavior continues, Ms. Campbell-Bertollo can certainly make Mario leave the library and go to the principal's office, but there will not be a record of set precedent.

Include, Grow | Family Interactions

The Situation: Reaching Beyond Barriers

Every couple of months, Clemencia, the school library assistant, sends home school library newsletters to school community members. Usually, the newsletters bring about increased circulation and participation in the library's creative programming. She rarely receives any correspondence back, although sometimes she gets questions about late fees. Her perspective changes when Rose, a regular visitor to the school library, stops by with a question. Rose tells Clemencia that she usually helps her father understand what is going on in the school library and social events at school by translating the newsletter and other materials that are sent home. Rose is nervous to share that sometimes she cannot accurately translate the materials, which leaves her father in the dark. She is worried that because her father does not read English, he may be missing valuable information about the places Rose enjoys, like the school library, which will make those places less important to him. Clemencia lets Rose know that all is well and not to worry. She also reassures the learner that she will think of a way to make the newsletter more inclusive for the Turkish families, a majority within the school community.

Internal Conflict

Clemencia has been given the responsibility of editing and sending out the quarterly newsletter. It is a short informational document, mostly used to highlight dates and useful resources available to learners and families. Clemencia is worried that translating the document, no matter how short, will take too long. She is also concerned about accurately translating her template because she has no familiarity with Turkish. Unsure whether translating the newsletter will make a difference in the lives of those in the school community, she reminds herself of Rose's poignant conversation.

What Is the Harm?

Clemencia knows that Rose's experience is not unique within the Turkish community in her district. Learners like Rose regularly carry the stressful responsibility of translating documents, important phone calls, appointment visits, and more for their family members. This duality of self, Rose at school and Rose at home, can strain the sense of belonging that is essential to growth in both environments. Although we cannot remove that stressor from her everyday life, we can try to alleviate the stress in at least one small area of her life, through the translation of school library documents. Her family will be able to see how important the school library is to her by seeing the great programs and resources in the newsletter, instead of simply being told about them. Rose and other learners whose families speak native languages other than English can benefit from the inclusion of their families within their safe space, the school library.

Strategies for Repairing the Climate

Clemencia can start by consulting the school librarian about providing families a translated version of the newsletter. If approved, she can take her already-made template and create a copy. Because she does not speak or read Turkish, she can rely on online translating tools to obtain an approximate translation of the small amount of text regularly found in her newsletter. After she edits her new copy of the Turkish version of the school library newsletter template, Clemencia can start looking outward for assistance. With support from the school librarian, she can look for a fellow educator, community leader, or public librarian who can read Turkish and is willing to proofread the quarterly newsletter during the school year. With the already-created approximate translation template document, the responsibilities of those assisting will be minimal, which will be more enticing given everyone's busy schedule. Likewise, as the general Turkish newsletter template is revised with the correct translation, Clemencia's time commitment regarding newsletter maintenance, in both English and Turkish, will be very similar to what it was before.

Explore, Grow | Staff Interaction

The Situation: Working through Resistance

Ms. Aviles is the school librarian for a library that is open to learners and educators most periods of the day. Throughout the day, Ms. Aviles sees learners and educators flood into the school library, using the space as a refuge, hangout, break room, resource center, and meeting space. She is taking her first steps in the culturally responsive journey, so there is not yet any signage or safe space climate in the school library. Mr. Khan, a fellow educator, visits the library every day. His routine is to come in, grab a seat near the librarian's desk, and converse loudly with Ms. Aviles throughout the period. Usually, the conversation relates to community news, but lately, Mr. Khan has been voicing inappropriate comments regarding gender, class, and race that are not conducive to creating a safe space for the learners who regularly use the school library.

Internal Conflict

Interpersonal communication is difficult in any workplace, but especially for school librarians. Our collaboration and learner engagement opportunities rely heavily on nurturing partnerships. Not wanting to burn any bridges, Ms. Aviles is nervous about approaching Mr. Khan about his topics of conversation. She is also aware that because she just recently began her culturally responsive journey, she does not have any signage, policy, or talking points to fall back on.

She does not want to alienate Mr. Khan, but she can easily see how the conversations shift toward microaggressions and harmful anecdotes that are hurtful to the nearby learners. She understands that Mr. Khan feels comfortable in the school library space, and she needs to find a way to continue to make him comfortable while also setting necessary boundaries.

What Is the Harm?

Whereas productive discourse focusing on gender, race, and class is valuable, microaggressions and stereotypical anecdotes are not. If we are building safe, culturally responsive school libraries, we want to make sure that there are boundaries to combat ignorance and hate in a civil way. Mr. Khan may not know that what he is saying is wrong because he has never been challenged or told otherwise. It is not Ms. Aviles's job to teach Mr. Khan, but it is Ms. Aviles's job to protect the learners who use the school library and the culture she wants to build and maintain.

According to Sue et al. (2007), there are three types of microaggressions:

> Microinsults: communications that convey rudeness and insensitivity and demean a person's identity. Microassaults: verbal or nonverbal attacks meant to hurt the intended victim through name-calling, avoidant behavior, or purposeful discriminatory actions. Microinvalidations: communications that exclude, negate, or nullify the psychological thoughts, feelings, or experiential reality of persons belonging to minority groups.

Huynh (2012) wrote,

> Even supposedly innocuous forms of discrimination are associated with elevated levels of anxiety, anger, and stress, which may increase feelings of depression and sickness. Microaggressions should be recognized as subtle discrimination that send messages about group status and devaluation, and like overt discrimination, can evoke powerful emotional reactions and may affect mental health.

Strategies for Repairing the Climate

Ms. Aviles can create and post signage that exemplifies the types of behavior that are encouraged in the school library space. She can also begin to write a draft of behavioral policy, which will outline in direct language the type of behavior that will not be tolerated. She can plan to send out photos of the space with signage clearly visible in the next newsletter with a link to information about norm creation and culturally responsive resources. Then she can address Mr. Khan with respect and clarity to explain that conversations, even seemingly innocuous and casual ones, need to follow the school library guidelines and be school appropriate. Ms. Aviles can explain to Mr. Khan that she does not appreciate certain anecdotes being told within the school library and does not agree with viewpoints that are harmful and stereotypical. To encourage valuable discourse, Ms. Aviles can invite Mr. Khan to share his perspectives outside school hours or during breaks where they can casually discuss their respective viewpoints guided by a civil and informed attitude.

Include, Think | Policy

The Situation: Trust and Support

School librarian Mx. Lee is working on the first steps of updating their school library policy. They read the existing bare-bones school library policy and made preliminary updates to language and formatting. They also created a small group of trusted learners and educators to participate in collaborative evaluation and adjustments. This is the first time they will oversee a small focus group, and they want to be able to lead the group with culturally responsive techniques and encourage open dialogue. They are unsure, however, how to dismantle power structures between learners and educators to promote an environment of respect and open communication right from the start of the process. This policy creation process will take time, even an entire school year, so they want to foster a positive relationship and atmosphere.

Internal Conflict

Mx. Lee regularly invites learners and other educators to participate and connect with the school library collection and creative programs throughout the year. Though they have facilitated creative endeavors between learners and educators, the power dynamics were not at the forefront of their concerns. Now that Mx. Lee is encouraging delicate and critical conversations between the two groups regarding library space and collection policies, they are acutely aware of communication breakdown.

What Is the Harm?

Communication breakdowns occur when participants feel like they are not heard, appreciated, or taken into consideration. Regardless of age, engaging in open dialogue that is rooted in themes of culture, race, class, and gender requires leaning into vulnerability, so proper care must be taken. Actions that lead to communication breakdown include assumptions, judgment, negativity, misinterpretations, and being closed-minded to new perspectives. It is impossible to guarantee that any of these actions will be avoided, but it is Mx. Lee's duty to minimize the possibility. As always, building respect and encouraging trust will be of the utmost importance.

Strategies for Expanding Perspectives

Mx. Lee can foster positive relationships between learners and educators by setting expectations and encouraging vulnerability during meetings. They can encourage learners and educators to step outside their comfort zones and their traditional, structured roles. Both groups of participants can be encouraged to take on the role of the other during discussions. Learners and educators can educate each other about their individual personal/professional experiences, their vision regarding the school library, and the aspects of policy that can reinforce a positive, culturally responsive, holistic environment.

To prepare the group to lean into vulnerability, Mx. Lee can set ground rules for participation and equip the group with a private virtual document for information sharing and feedback. In order to create ground rules for the group, they can build on the techniques they've learned like creating norms. As with the norms they encourage in their school library to foster a safe space for learners, they can create norms for the functional brave space within the focus group. Holman and Mejía (2019, n.p.) introduced the concept of brave spaces in "Safe Spaces, Brave Spaces and Why We Gon' Be Alright": "Brave spaces can look, sound, and feel different from one another, but the general idea is to cultivate a productive dialogue where participants are encouraged to speak honestly and critically from their own experience toward the end of mutual learning and liberation." Mx. Lee can adapt Holman and Mejía's brave space agreement examples to create their own agreement with set focus group norms. Ensuring that the participants in the focus group understand and agree to the norms at the start of each meeting will encourage adherence during discussions and critical evaluations of policy point ideas. From there, Mx. Lee can nurture the focus group's collaborative atmosphere and confront any breach of norms, as they normally would in their daily practice.

Deeper Understanding

The scenarios presented offer a practical view of the types of encounters we may have when we introduce and maintain culturally responsive practices in our lessons, spaces, and collaborations. They let us experience possible conflicts, understand the consequences associated with those conflicts, and work through solutions in a safe way. We must take several concepts into consideration while processing conflict, harm, and solutions. Every school community is different, but harm is not specific to any one culture, race, gender, class, or identity—it is a universal human experience. Although we cannot create and maintain a school library devoid of harmful experiences, we can try to be intentional in our efforts to encourage and empower learners and educators to work against harm and toward inclusion and inquiry. As modeled when explaining the harm that can stem from certain situations, equipping ourselves with data and resources pertaining to problems, before and after they arise, can assist us in addressing those problems or in justifying our actions to administrators. Our collection maintenance efforts, policy analysis, communication methods, and ability to address positive and negative situations as they arise will create valued momentum for enhancing our relationships and impact.

PART IV

Evaluation

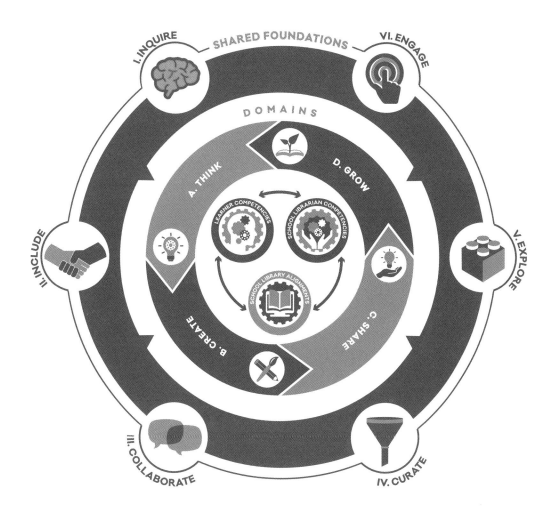

8

School Librarian Evaluation

As we approach the evaluation stages, take time to pause and admire the subtle shifts in consciousness that have manifested in your practice. Embracing vulnerability, though essential for this journey, is emotionally trying. Creating moments for intentional pause and reflection will help you work through the emotionally driven process thoughtfully and effectively. Along with pause and reflection is the implementation of evaluation. Evaluation, observation, and assessment are vital in our profession. They offer us opportunities to check in, reflect, and respond to feedback throughout the school year. We will explore self-evaluation and administrative evaluation methods and support materials to guide our process.

Self-Evaluation

We are familiar with outward examinations of our practices and spaces, but placing value on inward, critical examinations of those elements is not usually discussed outside our own heads. Self-evaluation builds on the inward reflection we worked through at the very start of this journey. Instead of reflecting on our personal identities and viewpoints, we will focus our reflections on our practices and school libraries. Be prepared to use the techniques learned, like buffing our critical culturally responsive lens and valuing intentional learner-centric mentality, while blending in the tools already present in our school librarian repertoire (figure 0.3, V.D.P1).

Before we start the emotional heavy lifting, let us ground ourselves. Introducing short moments of intentional, mindful breathing and sense awareness can help center you before, during, and after positive and negative situations, feedback, and evaluations. When focusing on self-evaluation, it is important to take a moment and remove ourselves from the outside stressors of our physical and mental spaces to look at things objectively.

CHALLENGE: LET'S GET GROUNDED

Try this quick meditation exercise whenever you have a moment to yourself.

Start with the breath. Take a deep breath in, and let it fill your belly. Exhale through your mouth, taking longer than you think you should. Repeat those intentionally long breaths four more times, without thinking about or doing anything else.

Next, whether you are standing or sitting, keep your breath work going while becoming mindful of your body. Start from the top of your body and travel downward. While taking relaxed breaths, soften your gaze or close your eyes, then relax your jaw and drop your shoulders and your arms. Let your arms swing gently at your sides, soften your hands, relax your stance so your knees are slightly bent, and wiggle your toes in your shoes. Keep your breath deep while you open and refocus your eyes and slowly rejoin your surroundings.

Most importantly, give yourself gratitude for including this moment of mindfulness in your day.

Our Priorities

After centering ourselves, we can begin to embrace reflection about and evaluation of our skills, practices, and spaces. Begin the evaluation process with the basics. Reflect on the professional goals set at the beginning of the school year. Think deeply about why we set those goals for ourselves. Were the goals in response to past setbacks, newly acquired knowledge, or changes in population needs? Were they set for you by leadership in your building? Our goals might be a combination of all these considerations. After analyzing the reasoning behind our goals, we can start to consider our emotional commitment and connection to those goals—the why. Why should we care about our goals? Where do our priorities lie?

Personally, I often see my goals as occupying two categories. I have goals set for me and goals that I set because of sparked interest or need. The ones set for me are institutional goals. These goals are based on district goals and might touch upon restorative practices, literacy, and pedagogical methods that I find myself having to translate into my school library practice. The projects and long-term goals that I set for myself are based on the patterns I observe in the school library, meaning that they are highly representative of my group of learners and therefore are at the forefront of my mind. When I think about my priorities, the goals that surround my craft and the school library are the goals that I think about daily.

For example, one of my goals was to create intentionally curated, culturally responsive book displays for the entire school year. Because I changed the display every couple of weeks, I planned out a rough outline for the year, knowing that those themes could change, depending on societal events and trends, and I kept an eye out for book titles that would be relevant to include. This type of creative, yearlong project attracted my attention once a day, even if only for five or ten minutes. Other goals, like district-wide initiatives on literacy, are implemented in our lessons and our collaborative partnerships with other educators. The priority level is still high and as important and impactful as the others, but these goals require less attention throughout the day. Instead, they may take up more of our mental space during specific times, like lesson planning and collaborative discussions.

Melding Practices

Fortunately, the American Association of School Librarians (AASL) provides us standards, competencies, and frameworks that offer direct language and guidance for evaluation of our practice. The *National School Library Standards* highlight valuable principles throughout learners' and our own journeys toward competence. AASL focuses its standards on being learner-centric and growth-minded, negating deficit thinking through acknowledging learner capabilities, scaffolding pedagogy, and enabling learner voice, choice, and agency. Nurturing the merger of the AASL Standards and culturally responsive work in our school libraries makes sense when our collective goal is to support learners' growth through personalized learning experiences. The *AASL Standards Frameworks Applied to Culturally Responsive Practice* (see figure 0.3) provides crossroads and connections between the AASL Standards Integrated Frameworks and the culturally responsive principles grounding our competencies in action. Practices and activities in the framework are meant to guide us and give us a scaffolded pathway when beginning and while continuing the journey toward creating and maintaining culturally responsive school libraries.

Assessing Our Mindset

In looking at our activities through the lens of culturally responsive practice, we can begin to think about where we were when we started the journey and where we are today. Our personal viewpoints, biases, and cultural backgrounds play large parts in our roles as school librarians. At this point, we should know more about our social identities and our personal identities as well as our biases. We should be able to recognize information that forms us culturally, like our tastes, values, stances, locations, upbringing, languages, and behaviors. We should also be able to recognize how our identity translates into our actions (figure 0.3, V.D.P2). While doing the inward work, we also explored outward, analyzing our instruction and our spaces.

Instruction

Our identity work and reflection allow us to create school libraries that are representative of a multitude of backgrounds and experiences. Our lessons should present learners with the same rich, inclusive educational discourse. Take a moment to reflect on your instruction methods. Are there areas dedicated to learner voice and choice? Are the examples and prompts provided throughout the lessons, assignments, and assessments inclusive of various cultural backgrounds and experiences? Are there opportunities for learner feedback without judgment or prejudice? These are questions that we should return to at least once every school year, if not more frequently. They provide us three solid, big-picture anchors to fall back on when evaluating our instruction practices.

Space

Turning our attention to our spaces offered us the opportunity to think critically about the visual messaging and access points within the school library. Because our spaces are representations of not only the learner but also ourselves, we should look at our spaces while performing a self-evaluation. How have our spaces evolved over time during this journey? Are there areas that are now more accessible to all learners, regardless of ability? Are signs and materials in languages or fonts that are accessible to learners? Are learners seeing themselves and their experiences represented in the library space? Did we make it easier for learners to feel like they can approach us about positive or negative experiences? As with the rest of the journey, spatial modifications cannot happen overnight because of budget and time, but with proper attention to smaller details, they can combine over time to create a sense of larger change.

Resources

Seeking resources within our professional community that can challenge and affirm our perspectives is essential to growth, especially in the evaluation process. Resources like the Wisconsin Department of Public Instruction's (2019) *Inclusive Services Assessment and Guide* can help you pinpoint the many areas in which evaluation can occur. The Inclusive Services Assessment is a thirty-page checklist with a glossary concerning governance, administration, staffing, collections, programming, services, facility, access, marketing, community engagement, funding, self-care for library workers, and inclusive culture at the library. Some points don't apply to the school library environment, but the points that are applicable align well with our culturally responsive work. The document also offers a more in-depth perspective on many inclusive services, which may guide you in areas that you are unfamiliar with or unaware of.

Administrative Evaluation

As school librarians, when not educating learners or maintaining our spaces, we are tasked with the never-ending need to prove our value and communicate our specific needs. During observation and evaluation cycles, those tasks are amplified. We have to not only showcase our unique skills as educators but also highlight our collection development and community outreach initiatives in ways that make sense for our school's teacher evaluation models. AASL offers helpful crosswalks to address the needs of school librarians within those rubrics, but we are pushing the boundaries of the competencies in those rubrics, for the better, by emphasizing a humanized and holistic approach to education and school library work. The reflective work we bring into our profession through the culturally responsive opportunities within this journey only builds upon the competencies and elements required from us at our baseline of performance.

Leaning on Standards

As we move forward, we should focus and lean on AASL's language and strategies for communicating with administrators in transparent and intentional ways. In the *National School Library Standards,* AASL states that "it is critical that school librarians have ongoing dialogue with the evaluating administrator about how the *AASL Standards Framework for School Librarians* aligns with the district evaluation document used for school librarians" (AASL 2018, 155). This ongoing dialogue relies on our knowledge of our school's evaluation documents, interpreting the frameworks that we want to integrate into our practices, understanding the format that works best for us and our evaluator, and collecting evidence of the practical application of the standards we are exhibiting.

Inviting Administrators Along on the Journey

When discussing our interest in culturally responsive practices with administrators, we must keep learner experience at the forefront of discourse. Although we know how essential our inward reflective work is and continues to be, highlighting the impact of culturally responsive work on learner instruction, social-emotional well-being, and school climate will encourage administrators to listen and learn. Equip yourself and your administrators with the resources and data points imparted in this book and found in the continuing research of practitioners in the field. Inviting administrators on our journey provides an opportunity to showcase not only our commitment to professional growth but also our commitment to bettering ourselves and strengthening our relationships within the school community.

Taking on the role of a culturally responsive leader, one who is not afraid to nurture vulnerability and challenge prejudicial situations, is a brave and necessary stance in our profession. You are modeling qualities like respect, open-mindedness, compassion, relevance, and emotional intelligence that can greatly impact your learners and their experiences in their school. They will see the school library space as a safe space where they can explore their intellectual and emotional needs within the pages of the books and the activities you provide. Support through this journey is essential, and finding that support system is not always easy. Inviting administrators into your space, your lessons, and your big-picture plans for the school library may seem daunting, but by doing so, you'll quickly recognize those who will support you and those who are not quite ready.

Embracing Your Growth

Feel empowered to share your personal professional goals regularly, and encourage administrators to make time for you to explain your rationale and highlight the great culturally responsive ideas and initiatives you plan on including in your practice throughout the school year. If you do not find the support you are looking for, continue working on your action steps and making them a priority and undeniably visible to your school community. Seemingly small changes, like signage, language use, norm creation, identity work, and book selection, have big impacts on daily school library operations. By embracing culturally responsive practices through the seeking and sharing of professional resources, you will find a community, inside or outside your school, that can support you and lend a hand in facilitating communication strategies with administrators. Your dedication to your practice will shine and have a contagious effect on those around you, inspiring growth.

9

Learner Evaluation

The comprehensive approach of culturally responsive instruction blends valuing learners' individual experiences, meeting their cultural and intrinsic needs, and setting high standards to emphasize rigor. Laying a culturally responsive foundation for our instruction allows us to better understand our learners and assess their learning on an individual level. Fortunately, there are various opportunities to assess learners within this instructional blend. By taking into consideration the *National School Library Standards*, district evaluation models, and the influence and integration of culturally responsive practices, we can assess learners through thoughtful and authentic methods.

Approachable Assessments

When focusing on the integration of culturally responsive strategies into assessments, try to keep it simple and intentional. Assessing learners based on qualitative data like identity work, reflection, and the application of their individual experiences should not add a burden to our usual methodology. Qualitative assessments offer opportunities for casual check-ins and focused, individualized moments of feedback. Please use the following as appropriate for your learners, while keeping an open mind about new concepts and techniques.

Reflection

Creating assessments using culturally responsive practices can be as simple as having learners participate in reflection opportunities. Reflection is a key component of both the learners' and our professional and personal growth. Each new concept and lesson offer an opportunity for learners to pause and reflect (figure 0.3, VI.D.P1). Guiding the learners through reflection and taking note of their responses provide us valuable information regarding their understanding of a topic, norm, concept, or assignment. Not only will learners gain an introspective approach when tackling new ideas, they will also see that their reflections matter. If reflection is brought into the instructional space intentionally before and after shifts in content or concepts, learners will become familiar with the process of taking stock of their preconceived notions, their knowledge and interest, and their growth throughout the course of study. This approach and skill set can follow them to other content areas and situations outside the school building. Aside from providing a heightened sense of introspection about what they are learning and why they are learning it, learners' reflections can offer valuable insights into their understanding and needs. Their input is vital and can shape the way that we form our lessons, participate in discussions, structure the school library space, and fortify their learning experience.

We can incorporate reflective exercises into many aspects of our instruction. If you are short of time because of curricular demands, try incorporating reflection as check-ins and exit tickets at the start and the end of the course period. Bookmarking lessons with reflection offers learners the opportunity to settle in, pause, and reflect on the prompt with a controlled set of guidelines and time limits. Offering different mediums for reflection may also liven up the introspection process. Online forms, slides, forums, or polls, for example, can provide learners a platform for reflection that they have not tried before. With that said, it is best to keep things simple and familiar, for the sake of time and our sanity. Because the prompts you create will guide learners toward quick reflection exercises, complexity may not be needed. Introduce reflection and find opportunities to incorporate it in a simple yet effective way that makes sense for your learners and your environment.

Introducing reflective practices within the school library, outside instruction, relies on creativity and engagement. No matter their age, learners yearn for creative outlets and expression. In my high school library, learners often participate in my passive arts and crafts station, themed guided prompts, and feedback methods. Providing learners seasonal coloring sheets and prompting them to share more about themselves and their upcoming goals, plans, and wishes works well in a flexibly scheduled school library environment. Having learners share their personal interests in these prompts and using those drawings, figures, sentiments, or blurbs to decorate the space provide a sense of community. Learners will see their artwork or goals displayed on one of the school library's walls, and they will know that their voice matters and is celebrated. Although not reflecting in an academic way, learners are being prompted to mindfully reflect on their past, present, and future through creativity. Similarly, amplifying learner voice through feedback methods can empower them to participate in advocacy efforts and the maintenance of school library culture. Prompting feedback through passive suggestion boxes, polls, online forms, or small advisory groups can inform change in the school library space based specifically on learner needs.

Formative Assessments

The *National School Library Standards* offer a guided structure for creating, grading, and applying formative assessments (AASL 2018, 132–141), so we will not reiterate their already thoughtful work. Instead, we can focus on the aspects of culturally responsive practice that we would like to include in our formative assessments and the way that we measure understanding and success in our learners. As important as the data we collect through formative assessments are, we must also shift the focus to ourselves when it comes to deliverables for learner success in understanding. Our instruction methods, though not necessarily in need of change, can benefit from a shift in mindset.

CHALLENGE: ASSESSMENT TASKS

Reflect on your go-to formative and summative assessment tasks. Choose four assessments to quickly evaluate. The assessments can range from casual check-ins to oral questions, quizzes, short-answer prompts, journal entries, or papers.

1. Are there areas within your assessments to include learner choice?
2. Are there areas within your assessments to include figures that are from varied cultural backgrounds and life experiences?
3. At the end of the assessment, during the feedback portion, what method of feedback is usually used? For example, is feedback presented through rubrics, comments, conversations, or a mix of many methods?
4. How often are learners able to respond to feedback or engage in conversations about redoing their work based on feedback?

Learning Partnerships

Referring to the foundations of culturally responsive teaching when addressing assessments brings us back to the teachings of Gay and Hammond. In *Culturally*

Responsive Teaching and the Brain, Hammond (2015, 88–89) stated, "According to Gay (2010), this is the ultimate goal of the culturally responsive teacher: to provide resources and personal assistance so students cultivate positive self-efficacy beliefs and a positive academic mindset." Hammond (2015, 89) went on to define *academic mindset* as "a student's attitudes, beliefs, and dispositions about school, learning, and his capacity as a learner that are associated with effort, perseverance, and positive academic achievement" (Snipes, Fanscali, & Stoker, 2012). Along with creating a space that uplifts learners and their voices, during instruction we should be guiding them toward academic success. Educators are led by curriculum standards and assessments. Because of curriculum demands and the increased momentum of the school year, it can be difficult to truly individualize learning, but keeping certain ideas in mind throughout the instruction process can set us up for valuable alliances with our learners in learning partnerships (figure 0.3, VI.B.A1).

Throughout this journey, trust is mentioned in many forms. We discussed trust relating to doing identity work, embracing vulnerability, and amplifying voices, but we also should look at trust as a key foundation of learner efficacy. Hammond (2015, 95) mentioned an alliance built upon three components: "the pact, teacher as ally, and the student as driver of his own learning." Within this structure, dependent learners who lack confidence in their own abilities and are falling behind are asked to embark on a reflective path alongside the educator to create a pact, or a formal agreement toward a learning goal, in a way that equalizes the power structure between learner and educator and that will "explicitly name what [the learner] intends to do as part of the partnership to meet this challenge" (96). Integrated in these foundations, particularly in the "teacher as ally" portion, are principles we have discussed throughout this journey, such as attention to verbal and nonverbal communication, high standards, emotional support, and reflection and feedback models.

A proper learner-educator partnership requires maintaining deliberately written, quality feedback combined with emotional support to foster change (figure 0.3, VI.B.P1). Hammond (2015, 101) wrote,

> Too often, culturally and linguistically diverse students who struggle have developed a set of learning moves that are not effective and they are not sure what's going wrong or what to do about it. They cannot do higher order thinking or complex work if they cannot learn to adjust their learning moves, acquire new ones, or strategize about how to tackle a task.

Addressing feedback, whether at the end of an assignment, during a discussion, or throughout a lesson, as a constructive conversation with the learner can promote a change in thinking and strategy. Using direct language and naming the problem assist in pinpointing the area in which the learner made a mistake and a clear path to correcting the behavior in the future. If we rely on advice or evaluative language, like "please add more examples" or "nice job on this paragraph," we are not giving learners the tools they need to modify their actions in the future in an actionable way that fits our expectations. Our language matters in ways that we cannot begin to understand. When learners fail to meet our expectations, it leads to a cycle of disappointment on our end and lack of self-confidence on their end. The partnership mentality urges us to communicate with learners effectively and compassionately, as we would with fellow educators in a collaborative setting. Building trust through actionable and clear feedback, offering emotional encouragement, and providing a space for learners to react to our feedback will move our relationships forward and increase efficacy in learner development.

Supplemental Standards

Learning for Justice, formally known as Teaching Tolerance, developed *Social Justice Standards: The Teaching Tolerance Anti-Bias Framework* (2018). The *Social Justice Standards* "recognize that, in today's diverse classrooms, students need knowledge and skills related to both prejudice reduction and collective action" (2). In this framework are four domains—Identity, Diversity, Justice, and Action—and five anchor standards within each domain. The framework is divided into four categories for the appropriate grade-level bands: K–2, 3–5, 6–8, and 9–12. Each grade-level band offers twenty distinct outcomes and scenarios in response to the domain and anchor standards. This framework will prove to be a valuable tool in your toolbox as you begin to form your evaluations around individual learner growth and reflective practices alongside the curriculum requirements.

Many of the standards and outcomes presented in the framework can be the product of the culturally responsive strategies and scenarios we have familiarized ourselves with on this journey. Some of the standards and outcomes, especially in the 9–12 grade-level band, expand on the concepts to promote intentional antibias accountability and action against exclusion, prejudice, and injustice. Within the grade-level outcomes in the *Social Justice Standards*, we see concepts that we can promote in our spaces, such as the following:

- ID.3-5.4: I can feel good about my identity without making someone else feel badly about who they are.
- DI.3-5.9: I feel connected to other people and know how to talk, work and play with others even when we are different or when we disagree.
- AC.3-5.17: I know it's important for me to stand up for myself and for others, and I know how to get help if I need ideas on how to do this.
- JU.9-12.15: I can identify figures, groups, events and a variety of strategies and philosophies relevant to the history of social justice around the world (2018, 6–7, 11).

Even if we do not explicitly refer to the frameworks in our curriculum evaluation, administrative observations, or our lesson plans, they can effectively influence our actions and guide our own growth and that of the school library. We can use this framework, in conjunction with the *AASL Standards Frameworks Applied to Culturally Responsive Practice* (see figure 0.3), to set up conceptual guidelines when we evaluate our services, spaces, and individual learner experiences and academic efficacy.

Purposeful Partnerships

Taking our toolbox with us when we collaborate with other educators allows us to maintain our momentum while also increasing our impact. Inviting educators into the school library and into collaborative experiences means melding two minds to create lessons and assessments that will benefit both parties. It also exposes new sets of learners and educators to the offerings of the school library. Approaching these opportunities with the same mindset as we approach our lessons and our spaces is essential to continue modeling our culturally responsive initiative and appropriately assessing learners based on that mindset. When we invite others into a conversation regarding collaborative opportunities, we must be transparent about our needs. Of course, the result of the collaboration should be positive and show knowledge gained by our learners, but we want the beginning of the collaboration to hold equal value (figure 0.3, VI.C.P2).

For example, if we always begin our lessons with a brief explanation of expected behavior and discussion norms, then we should make that practice evident to the collaborating educator. We want to follow the same successful patterns with that educator's class as we would with learners in our school libraries. Explaining to the educator the value you place on sharing norms and the speed with which the explanation can occur, as well as sharing benefits that you have witnessed during learner discussions, can help validate your stance and request. The same goes for any desire that follows the path of culturally responsive school libraries. Aspects of lesson planning and assessment creation that may be worth noting and that can be applied to several different subject areas are norm creation, learner voice, participating in group work with assigned roles, presenting finished products with peers as a shared learning environment, constructive and actionable feedback, and, of course, inclusive and responsive book selection.

We want to make sure that what we are doing within the school library walls continues in our actions in other learner spaces in the school community. We should look at collaborative experiences as an opportunity to model new perspectives and share new findings to enhance instruction as appropriate. It is common for us to feel like we are supplementary in the lessons of others, but in fact, if we are being asked to participate in the planning and execution of the lesson, then we matter. Our opinions matter, and our needs within the educational space matter. Transparent communication from the beginning can help foster productive partnerships and lead to more intentional assessments and meaningful results to guide learner efficacy.

CONCLUSION

Together, we have explored chapter after chapter of interpretation and integration strategies of culturally responsive practices specifically centered in school library settings. Throughout this journey, we dedicated time to looking inward, reflecting on our own identities, values, biases, and privileges, and to looking outward, evaluating our spaces and policies to promote inclusivity and growth. This vital work will continue long after you close this book. Think of this guide as a source of encouragement to keep learning and trying new things, not a checklist or finish line. To be an educator, a librarian, and a practitioner is to embrace continued learning. As I stated in the introduction, you are taking ownership of your profession, the role you play in your school, and, as a result, the impact you have on the lives of learners. Pause for a moment to practice gratitude toward yourself and your ability to grow personally and professionally.

Responding to the various cultural needs of our learners and their communities is only the beginning of the journey. Aside from learning more about ourselves and the ways in which we can promote inclusion and antibias in our libraries, we were also challenged to dig deeper into our knowledge and reasoning regarding race, gender, and class. These concepts are not unique to school libraries and require proper attention when addressed. Working toward a deeper understanding and proactive approaches to combat hate, injustice, and prejudice will continue to pave the way for learning and intentional change.

Maintain Momentum

Unlike the many iterations of hot-button issues that get worked and reworked, pushed on educators, and turnkeyed for every classroom, culturally responsive practices intentionally weave us into their fabric. Although we may find ourselves having to integrate other educational initiatives into our school library work, we can continue to prioritize identity work, intentional reflection opportunities, antibias policies, and the maintenance of responsive collections and spaces. Maintaining momentum

FIGURE C.1

S.H.A.R.P.E.N. your skills for culturally responsive practice

 SEEK RESOURCES: Lean on professional organizations and networks to gather information. By signing up for newsletters, resources will be pushed into your inbox. Professional organizations offer webinar recordings, booklists, updated articles, virtual meetings, and a built-in system of support.

 HONOR DIFFERENCES: Honor differences in identities and perspectives both cultural and societal in your professional work to ensure an objective view of the resources gathered and shared with educators and learners. Appreciate and encourage the individual background and skills that learners bring to school-based assignments and interactions by providing opportunities for peer-to-peer learning and creativity.

 ANALYZE DATA: Private- and public-school data are available for our analysis. School data amplify the importance of an inclusive and responsive environment by providing valuable insight through demographic facts. This type of information can inform your collection, services, and community's needs.

 REFLECT AUTHENTICALLY: Regularly pausing for reflection will offer a respite from the busy work environment and help ground yourself before and after educational feats. Guide learners through reflective exercises in which they can authentically explore their points of view, evaluate their prior knowledge, and assess their progress.

 PRACTICE TRANSPARENCY: Transparency acts as an invitation to learners, fellow educators, and administrators to support, promote, and advocate for the school library. Practice sharing policy, expectations, initiatives, and offerings with the school community to expand reach and understanding.

 EMBRACE VULNERABILITY: Vulnerability in our school libraries is contagious. Share with learners some personal aspects of your life or even common missteps you have encountered, and learners will reciprocate. Practice vulnerability during reflective exercises or whole-class discussions to create an environment that encourages sharing, compassion, and respect.

 NURTURE DIALOGUE: Dialogue has many modes and even more advantages. Prepare learners to discuss by creating and maintaining norms, promote opportunities for casual dialogue to embrace differing ideas and perspectives, and prompt learners with constructive and responsive feedback.

entails embracing new concepts and nurturing routines that benefit our learners and our profession. These opportunities can take different forms in each of our roles and spaces. They can also be dependent on our school's leadership and the morale in our buildings. Safeguarding our efforts through policy, transparency, accountability, and advocacy when communicating with administrators and community members will benefit our continued learning.

Continue to share resources that resonate and will impact your practice with fellow educators. As valuable as it is to share resources with and for learners, we should also attempt to supplement our colleagues' professional practice through our research and firsthand experiences as appropriate. Becoming an informational asset to your professional learning community will permit you to prioritize time for research and share your insights with others of similar interest. Learning communities not only enhance relationships within the school community but also provide a sounding board for ideas and perspectives regarding possible successes and failures of new techniques in the classroom and school library. By fostering relationships with those who share an interest in this work, you will find the support to continue to challenge yourself and the services you provide for learners. If you travel the road of culturally responsive practices alone, just know that you will not be alone for long. If you cannot find others in your building, seek outside your comfort zone and participate in larger networks. You stepped off your library island by embracing these methods, and you will find others along the way.

The concepts and strategies presented in this guide have the potential to bring impactful, mindful, and intentional change to our profession and our spaces. Setting aside time to explore the benefits of integrating culturally responsive practices and inclusivity into your school library shows that you prioritize learners' experience and place value in their growth. Continue S.H.A.R.P.E.N.-ing your skills long after closing this book (figure C.1). You will find what feels right, what works and does not work, and what you are willing to stand behind as you advocate for your school library and your learners. You may also find yourself challenged by others once you start intentionally working toward an inclusive atmosphere. As always, resources, data, and an open mind are your greatest tools against exclusion.

Embrace new methods and give yourself grace when trying them. There is no end to these practices, so there are plenty of opportunities for failure and success along the way. If we fail at trying to do better for our spaces and our learners, we are still on the right course and should try again. Realize your potential for growth and humanity. Address problematic interactions and regressions with haste and intention. Know that support exists outside your school library walls and that inspiration can stem from anywhere. Most importantly, make time for your own reflective practices. We cannot serve if we have nothing to give, so take care of yourself. It will directly translate into your craft. Thank you for joining me on this journey. I look forward to seeing the great work we do together.

APPENDIX A

Social Identity Garden Worksheet

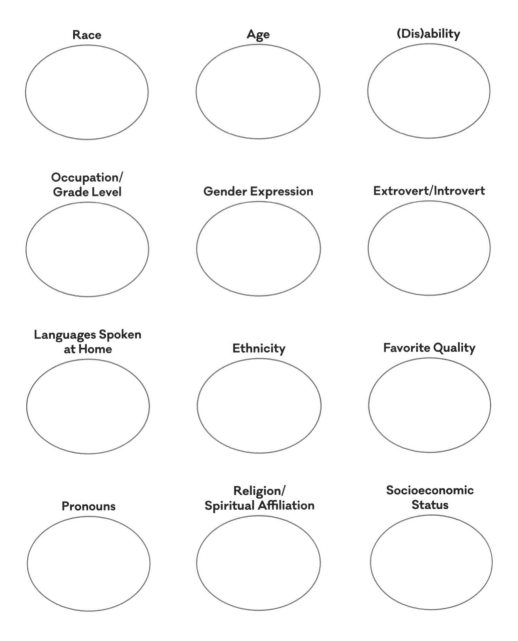

Race

Age

(Dis)ability

Occupation/
Grade Level

Gender Expression

Extrovert/Introvert

Languages Spoken
at Home

Ethnicity

Favorite Quality

Pronouns

Religion/
Spiritual Affiliation

Socioeconomic
Status

APPENDIX B

Personal Identity Garden Worksheet

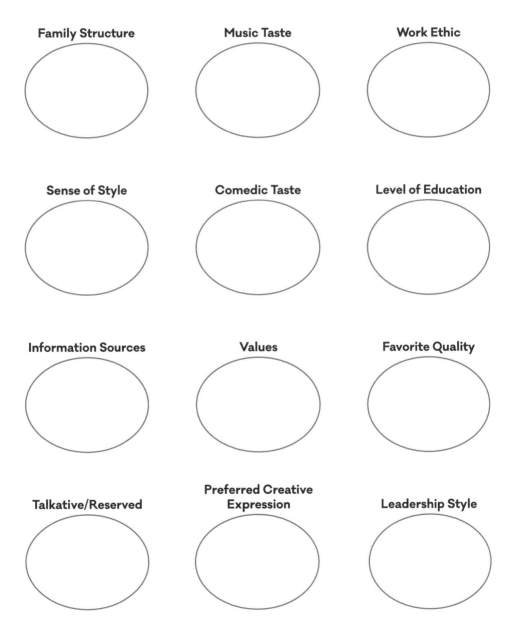

Family Structure

Music Taste

Work Ethic

Sense of Style

Comedic Taste

Level of Education

Information Sources

Values

Favorite Quality

Talkative/Reserved

Preferred Creative
Expression

Leadership Style

APPENDIX C

KWWHL Chart Worksheet

TOPIC:

What do you *know*?	
***Why* do you know about the topic?**	
What do you *want* to know?	
***How* will you find information?**	
What have you *learned*?	

WORKS CITED

AASL American Association of School Librarians. 2018. *National School Library Standards for Learners, School Librarians, and School Libraries*. Chicago: ALA Editions.

Alim, H. Samy, and Django Paris. 2017. "What Is Culturally Sustaining Pedagogy and Why Does It Matter?" In *Culturally Sustaining Pedagogies: Teaching and Learning for Justice in a Changing World*, edited by Django Paris and H. Samy Alim. New York: Teachers College Press.

Anderson, Monica, and Andrew Perrin. 2018. "Nearly One-in-Five Teens Can't Always Finish Their Homework Because of the Digital Divide." Pew Research Center. pewresearch.org/fact-tank/2018/10/26/nearly-one-in-five-teens-cant-always-finish-their-homework-because-of-the-digital-divide/.

Brown, P. 1991. "Passing: Differences in Our Public and Private Self." *Journal of Multicultural Social Work* 1:33–50.

Bucher, Katherine T., and KaaVonia Hinton-Johnson. 2013. *Young Adult Literature: Exploration, Evaluation, and Appreciation*. 3rd ed. Pearson.

Center for Culturally Proficient Educational Practice. 2020. "The Continuum." ccpep.org/home/what-is-cultural-proficiency/the-continuum/.

Gay, Geneva. 2002. "Preparing for Culturally Responsive Teaching." *Journal of Teacher Education* 53, no. 2: 106–16. doi.org/10.1177/0022487102053002003.

———. 2010. "Culturally Responsive Teaching: Theory, Research, and Practice." New York: Teachers College Press.

GLSEN. n.d. *Safe Space Kit: A Guide to Supporting Lesbian, Gay, Bisexual, Transgender, and Queer Students in Your School*. glsen.org/sites/default/files/2019-11/GLSEN%20English%20SafeSpace%20Book%20Text%20Updated%202019.pdf.

———. 2022. "About Us." Accessed 2022. www.glsen.org/about-us.

Hammond, Zaretta. 2015. *Culturally Responsive Teaching and the Brain: Promoting Authentic Engagement and Rigor among Culturally and Linguistically Diverse Students*. Thousand Oaks, CA: Corwin.

Holman, Felicia, and Ellie Mejía. 2019. "Safe Spaces, Brave Spaces and Why We Gon' Be Alright." City Bureau. citybureau.org/notebook/2019/12/19/safe-spaces-brave-spaces-and-why-we-gon-be-alright.

Huynh, V. W. 2012. "Ethnic Microaggressions and the Depressive and Somatic Symptoms of Latino and Asian American Adolescents." *Journal of Youth and Adolescence* 41 (7): 831–46. doi.org/10.1007/s10964-012-9756-9.

Kanuha, Valli Kalei. 1999. "The Social Process of 'Passing' to Manage Stigma: Acts of Internalized Oppression or Acts of Resistance?" *Journal of Sociology and Social Welfare* 26 (4): 27–46. scholarworks.wmich.edu/jssw/vol26/iss4/3.

Ladson-Billings, Gloria. 2014. "Culturally Relevant Pedagogy 2.0: A.k.a. the Remix." *Harvard Educational Review* 84, no. 1 (Spring): 74–84, 135. proquest.com/scholarly-journals/culturally-relevant-pedagogy-2-0-k-remix/docview/1511014412/se-2.

Learning for Justice. 2016. *Reading Diversity: A Tool for Selecting Diverse Texts*. Extended Edition. learningforjustice.org/sites/default/files/2017-11/Reading-Diversity-v2-Redesign-WEB-Nov2017.pdf.

———. 2018. *Social Justice Standards: The Teaching Tolerance Anti-Bias Framework.* Montgomery, AL: Learning for Justice. learningforjustice.org/sites/default/files/2020-09/TT-Social-Justice-Standards-Anti-bias-framework-2020.pdf.

Lindsey, Randall B., Kikanza Nuri-Robins, Raymond D. Terrell, and Delores B. Lindsey. 2019. *Cultural Proficiency: A Manual for School Leaders*. Thousand Oaks, CA: Corwin.

Nuri-Robins, Kikanza, Delores B. Lindsey, Randall B. Lindsey, and Raymond D. Terrell. 2012. *Culturally Proficient Instruction: A Guide for People Who Teach*. Thousand Oaks, CA: Corwin.

Paris, Django. 2012. "Culturally Sustaining Pedagogy: A Needed Change in Stance, Terminology, and Practice." *Educational Researcher* 41 (3): 93–97. doi.org/10.3102/0013189X12441244.

Snipes, J., C. Fancsali, C., and G. Stoker. 2012. *Student Academic Mindset Interventions*. San Francisco: Stupski Foundation.

Staats, Cheryl. 2012. "Implicit Bias and (Mis)Perceptions." Kirwan Institute for the Study of Race and Ethnicity. April 10, 2012. kirwaninstitute.osu.edu/article/implicit-bias-and-misperceptions.

Sue, D. W., C. M. Capodilupo, G. C. Torino, J. M. Bucceri, A. M. B. Holder, K. L. Nadal, and M. Esquilin. 2007. "Racial Microaggressions in Everyday Life: Implications for Clinical Practice." *American Psychologist* 62 (4): 271–86. doi.org/10.1037/0003-066X.62.4.271.

Tyner, Madeline. 2020. "The Numbers Are In: 2019 CCBC Diversity Statistics." *CCBlogC* (blog). June 16. ccblogc.blogspot.com/2020/06/the-numbers-are-in-2019-ccbc-diversity.html.

Villegas, Ana María, and Tamara Lucas. 2002. "Preparing Culturally Responsive Teachers: Rethinking the Curriculum." *Journal of Teacher Education* 53 (1): 20–32. doi.org/10.1177/0022487102053001003.

Wisconsin Department of Public Instruction. 2019. *The Inclusive Services Assessment and Guide.* dpi.wi.gov/sites/default/files/imce/libraries/Publib/Inclusive-Services/Inclusive_Services_Assessment_and_Guide_for_Wisconsin_Public_Libraries_2019_updated_Sept.pdf.

ADDITIONAL READING

"Culturally Responsive-Sustaining Education Framework." n.d. New York State Education Department. nysed.gov/common/nysed/files/programs/crs/culturally-responsive -sustaining-education-framework.pdf.

"Effective Communication: Barriers and Strategies." n.d. Centre for Teaching Excellence, University of Waterloo. Accessed November 12, 2021. uwaterloo.ca/centre-for -teaching-excellence/teaching-resources/teaching-tips/communicating-students/ telling/effective-communication-barriers-and-strategies.

Gay, Geneva, and Kipchoge Kirkland. 2003. "Developing Cultural Critical Consciousness and Self-Reflection in Preservice Teacher Education." *Theory Into Practice* 42, no. 3: 181–87. doi.org/10.1207/s15430421tip4203_3.

Honma, Todd. 2005. "Trippin' Over the Color Line: The Invisibility of Race in Library and Information Studies." *InterActions: UCLA Journal of Education and Information Studies* 1 (2). doi.org/10.5070/d412000540.

Kumasi, Kafi D., and Renee F. Hill. 2019. "What Does Cultural Competence Mean to Preservice School Librarians? A Critical Discourse Analysis." In *Social Justice and Cultural Competency: Essential Readings for School Librarians*, edited by Marcia A. Mardis and Dianne Oberg, 64–75. Santa Barbara, CA: Libraries Unlimited.

McNaughton, D., D. Hamlin, J. McCarthy, D. Head-Reeves, and M. Schreiner. 2008. "Learning to Listen: Teaching an Active Listening Strategy to Preservice Education Professionals." *Topics in Early Childhood Special Education*, 27, 223–31.

Meeks, Amanda. 2017. "Cultivating Courage in Our Professions and Communities (w/ Brave Spaces)." *Thoughts on Libraries and Art and Life, Oh My* (blog). November 14. outspokinandbookish.wordpress.com/2017/11/14/cultivating-courage-in-our -professions-and-communities-w-brave-spaces/.

Sheets, Rosa Hernandez. 2009. "What Is Diversity Pedagogy?" *Multicultural Education* 16 (3): 11. Gale Academic OneFile. link.gale.com/apps/doc/A205495607/AONE?u =anon~6563c478&sid=googleScholar&xid=118c7dc9.

Sonnie, Amy. n.d. "Advancing Racial Equity in Public Libraries: Case Studies from the Field" (Issue Brief). Government Alliance on Race and Equity. Accessed September 2021. racialequityalliance.org/resources/advancing-racial-equity-in-public-libraries -case-studies-from-the-field/.

"2021 Update to ALA's Core Competences of Librarianship." 2021. Committee on Education. ala.org/educationcareers/2021-update-alas-core-competences-librarianship#:~:text=The%20ALA%20Core%20Competences%20(ALACCs,early%20in%20a%20library%20career.

Weger, H., Jr., G. R. Castle, and M. C. Emmett. 2010. "Active Listening in Peer Interviews: The Influence of Message Paraphrasing on Perceptions of Listening Skill." *International Journal of Listening* 24:34–49.

Yeager, David Scott, Valerie Purdie-Vaughns, Julio Garcia, Nancy Apfel, Patti Brzustoski, Allison Master, William T. Hessert, Matthew E. Williams, and Geoffrey L. Cohen. 2014. "Breaking the Cycle of Mistrust: Wise Interventions to Provide Critical Feedback across the Racial Divide." *Journal of Experimental Psychology: General* 143 (2): 804–24. doi.org/10.1037/a0033906.

INDEX

L

Ladson-Billings, Gloria, xii

language
  direct language in norms, 52, 53
  direct language in signage, 35–36
  in elementary school scenario, 61–63
  of feedback for learner, 84–85
  in high school scenario, 65–66
  of school library newsletter, 66–68
  in school library policy, 18–19
  Spanish-language titles, 28

late fees, 18

learner evaluation
  approachable assessments, 81
  Assessment Tasks challenge, 83
  formative assessments, 83
  learning partnerships, 83–85
  purposeful partnerships, 86–87
  reflection, 81–83
  supplemental standards for, 85–86

learner identity
  learner identity gardens, 54–55
  norms for discussions about, 5–6

learner voice
  See voice

learners
  AASL Standards Frameworks applied to
    culturally responsive practice, xx–xxvii
  affirming attitude toward, xvii
  brave space, creation of, 39
  choice, highlighting, 58
  class culture, 52, 54
  collaborating creatively with, 15–17
  collection access across platforms/
    spaces/abilities, 29–30
  cultural memberships and, 11
  culturally responsive practice and, xix
  culturally responsive teachers and, xvii
  in elementary school scenario, 61–63
  in family interactions scenario, 66–68
  in high school scenario, 65–66
  identities of, 54–55
  instruction methods, evaluation of, 78
  instructor role of school librarians, 51
  KWWHL Chart, 55, 56
  in library policy scenario, 70–71
  in middle school scenario, 63–64

  mindful modeling for leading learners,
    13–14
  needs, anticipation of, 15
  Norm Breach challenge, 53
  norms, creation of, 4–6
  partnerships with public libraries for,
    45–46
  readers' advisory networks, expanding,
    23–24
  representing learners' experiences, 42
  research strategies, reflecting on, 55–58
  safe space for, 38
  school librarian/affinity groups
    partnership, 44–45
  school library as safe space, 80
  school library collection for, 26, 28–29
  school library policy and, 17–19
  shared learning, 58–59
  signage for, evaluation of, 35–36

learning community, 91

learning experiences, shared
  from instruction, 14
  school library for, 58–59

Learning for Justice
  *Reading Diversity: A Tool for Selecting
    Diverse Texts*, 29
  safe space, school library as, 38
  Social Justice Standards, 85–86

learning partnerships, 83–85

"Learning to Listen: Teaching an Active
  Listening Strategy to Preservice Education
  Professionals" (McNaughton, Hamlin,
  McCarthy, Head-Reeves, & Schreiner),
  101

lenses
  critical lens for digital resources analysis,
    15
  exploring layers of, 11
  seeing school library space through
    critical lens, 35–36
  understanding, 12

Let's Get Grounded challenge, 76

LGBTQ+ community
  partnership with affinity groups, 44
  representation in school library
    collection, 25
  safe space, school library as, 38